COFFEE BASICS

Coffee Basics

A QUICK AND EASY GUIDE

Kevin Knox
Julie Sheldon Huffaker

JOHN WILEY & SONS, INC.
New York / Chichester / Brisbane / Toronto / Singapore

This text is printed on acid-free paper.

This publication is designed to provide accurate and
authoritative information in regard to the subject
matter covered. It is sold with the understanding that
the publisher is not engaged in rendering legal, accounting,
or other professional services. If legal advice or other
expert assistance is required, the services of a competent
professional person should be sought.

Library of Congress Cataloging-in-Publication Data:
Knox, Kevin.
     Coffee basics : a quick and easy guide / Kevin Knox, Julie Sheldon
Huffaker.
          p.   cm.
     Includes index.
     ISBN 0–471–13617–4 (pbk. : alk. paper)
     1. Coffee.   I. Huffaker, Julie Sheldon, 1967–   . II. Title.
TX415.K56   1996   96–5936
641.3'373--dc20

The coffee cup appearing on page 97 and elsewhere throughout the book, ©1993 by
Allegro Coffee Company, was created by Vermillion Designs and appears courtesy of
Allegro Coffee Company.

The following illustrations were created by Steve Katagiri, Katagiri Illustration &
Design: coffee branch and coffee cherry cross-section (page 9); scoop, water, and clock
(basic brewing equation, page 97); manual drip brewer (page 104); and home espresso
machine (page 129).

Printed in the United States of America

10 9 8 7 6

C O N T E N T S

PREFACE

Many volumes on coffee have been written, including a few that merit designation as classics. With all of these publications available and more glossy coffee-table tomes than one can set a cup upon, is there truly need for yet one more book on the subject?

Our affirmative answer to this question is a book that— to a greater degree than its predecessors— attempts to break down the barriers that exist between the world of the coffee professional and that of the consumer. Our goal is to walk readers down an unswerving path to superlative coffee. We want you to know the unvarnished truth: What's out there that's great? What's called great, but isn't? Why do some of the most popular brewing methods give you the least value for your dollar?

Between the two of us, we have roasted and brewed a great deal of coffee over the past twenty years. We've had the privilege of talking with customers at every level of sophistication. And, as we interact with an ever widening world of coffee drinkers, we're struck by the perceptual gulf between the customers who buy good coffee and the professionals whose lives revolve around it. Taste is ultimately a subjective matter. The road that leads there, however, is as objective as asphalt and full of pitfalls. There are basic truths governing the ability of a region to grow good coffee and of a roaster to sculpt its taste. There are coffees that have been processed well and those that have not, and there are straightforward formulas that yield exponentially better coffee than most consumers currently brew at home. We want to talk about these in accessible detail, and share with you some secrets for getting the most pleasure out of every coffee dollar you spend.

Since one of this book's authors buys and roasts coffee for a living, one might well question the inherent subjectivity of the text. Before you turn to page 1, we wish to make this abundantly clear: Despite the objectivity of much of the information presented, our overall approach to fine coffee is obstinately, passionately subjective. How could it possibly be any other way and still possess meaning?

The world of fine coffee is closely aligned with that of the exacting wine maker or accomplished chef. Fine coffee is unequivocally subjective in nature, a question of taste. Artisan roasters and brewers are tastemakers, distinguished by the informed personal stamp they lend to their products. As an enlightened consumer, your task is to seek out sources and brewing methods for your coffees whose respective preferences and emphasis most closely match your own.

Additionally, we want to demystify some of the more behind-the-scenes issues that make their way into the cup: Where issues such as decaffeination processes, organic coffees, coffee worker's rights, and world market pricing are concerned, what is the buzz all about?

There are basics, and there are beyond-basics; in all honesty, we've not stopped ourselves from providing a healthy amount of both. We believe that the more you know about coffee, the more you will enjoy each encounter with it. In an attempt to save you from being completely overwhelmed, however, we have tried to curb ourselves from presenting overly exhaustive detail.

American coffee pioneer George Howell moves through life with the motto, "In search of the ultimate cup," proffering an invitation to participate in a quest that has a beginning but, truly, no end. We hope that *Coffee Basics* will contribute significantly to expanding your horizons.

ACKNOWLEDGMENTS

While this is a relatively short book, the acknowledgment of all who have contributed to making it possible could easily reach chapter length.

My foremost debt is to my friend and co-author Julie Sheldon Huffaker. Her perceptiveness, sensitivity, writing skills, and love for the cultures from which coffee springs turned what could have been an esoteric project, of interest only to trade insiders, into a book that stands firmly on the consumer's side of the counter.

My wife, Erin, has borne the weight of being a "book widow" with grace and endless support.

Professional debts run wide and deep: I can hardly imagine another industry so full of passionate, talented people. Jeffrey Cohn, founder and chairman of Allegro Coffee Company, gave me my first opportunities in coffee and has been a friend and mentor for nearly 20 years. Terry Tierney, president of Allegro, has also been a key mentor and supporter, and he, along with our roasting and quality control staff, made it possible for me to take time to write.

Jerry Baldwin and Jim Reynolds, both of Peet's Coffee and Tea, taught and continue to teach others who love coffee what quality without compromise is all about; without their example, I would never have found a career in coffee. Expert roasters Steve Smith, Michael Dice, and Tom

Walters showed me how to turn dedication to excellence into a cooling tray of delicious proof.

On another coast, and at another roast, lives George Howell, founder of Boston's Coffee Connection and one of the coffee world's most knowledgeable and passionate spokesmen. I know of no one who has done more to improve the quality of American coffee, and no one has taught me more, both directly and by example.

Howard Schultz and Dave Olsen, both of Starbucks, gave me the opportunity to cram several decades worth of growth and learning into a few short years in Seattle. Seattle is also the home of pioneering espresso machine importer and manufacturer Kent Bakke of Espresso Specialists, from whom I continue to learn much about coffee and life, and their particular Italian inextricability.

Green coffee growers, importers, and exporters also contributed mightily to the educational process from which this book springs. I owe special thanks to my multitalented green-coffee broker/writer/connoisseur friend Tim Castle, of Castle and Company.

The list of farmers who have contributed great coffees and learning opportunities could itself fill a small book, but I am especially indebted to Bill McAlpin of Hacienda La Minita for his generous education regarding the complex and subtle relationships between farming practices and final cup quality.

I'm also indebted to the following green-coffee importers for great learning opportunities and great coffees: Alan Odom and Alan Nietlisbach of Holland Coffee; Erna Knutsen at Knutsen Coffees, Michael Glenister of Amcafé; Robert Fullmer at Royal Coffee; Mohamed Moledina of

Moledina Commodities; Jeremy Woods of American Coffee; and Wolfgang Dehner of List & Beisler.

—*Kevin Knox*

At the risk of plagiarizing my co-author's work, I feel compelled to return the initial sentiments of his acknowledgments in kind. Years ago, when I first began working as a *barista* for Starbucks Coffee Company, Kevin took the time to meet with me on the strength of an impassioned letter. Over one of his exquisite and legendary dinners, he invited me to discuss coffee at length—and this book is evidence of the delightful fact that our conversation never ended.

For every thoughtful word and priceless exchange, I thank him. Kevin's extraordinary, fearless intelligence and keen sensitivity drive a relentless pursuit of quality. The coffee industry is lucky indeed that he has chosen it.

My superlative partner, Leslie Bevan, has cheered and cooked and cosseted throughout the process of this book with unfathomable generosity. For this, and for her insistence that I maintain some perspective broader than the width of my computer screen, I am deeply, joyfully grateful.

I want to thank other players in the coffee world who have indelibly shaped my experience there and beyond: an earlier Starbucks crew—John Plymale, Doug Rimbach, Paul Sorensen, Suzanne, and Eva; Gay Niven, Paul Evanson, Alex Jones, Lisa McCrummen, and Brandy Poirier—whose wit, wisdom, and willingness to grow made days on the job (and days since) very, very good. Humble appreciation is extended to the customers whose questions stimulated my own learning—and especially to Merris Sumrall, who continues to ask more than most. Fierce gratitude to the maverick colony of experts at Espresso Specialists in Seattle for their unflinching championing of coffee quality; for taking time to answer my questions, kindly; and for practicing a necessary but all too rare brand of vocational humanism. And many thanks to Liz Mangelsdorf for her generous permission to reprint the stunning origin photos which grace several pages in Chapter 1.

Doug MacKinnon and my ever-supportive mother, Susan, paid thoughtful attention to the questions I asked and the chapters I sent. Their comments were useful, kind, and definitive proof that love is enough to get the manuscript back on time.

Finally, sincere appreciation to Cathy Brown, indexing lioness, for her ebullient nature and wide-ranging talents; and to the skilled and personable professionals at John Wiley & Sons—particularly Claire Thompson and Maria Colletti—for dedicating so much positive energy to this project.

Thank you all.

—Julie Sheldon Huffaker

What Is Coffee?

To develop a knowledgeable relationship with coffee—and particularly to learn to distinguish and appreciate its flavors—one must first understand what coffee is. The coffee bean is actually the seed, or pit, of the round, red "cherry" fruit of a tropical evergreen shrub. The coffee shrub grows up to 15 feet in height, and its branches grow thick with broad, waxy green leaves. In addition to the claret red clusters of coffee cherries, each coffee branch offers an abundance of luxuriant, jasmine-scented flowers.

A normal cherry contains two seeds, or beans, that grow nestled against each other. When one of these beans doesn't develop properly, the remaining bean takes over the extra space at the heart of the cherry and becomes unusually rounded. These anomalies are known as "peaberries." Because of their unique appearance, they are occasionally sorted out from the other beans and sold separately.

Today, most of us consume our coffee by the cup: processed to free the seeds from the cherry, roasted to enhance the flavors locked inside, ground finely, and brewed with fresh, hot water. Earlier devotees, however, fermented the tangy coffee fruit for liquor; there is also evidence to show they boiled the leaves for tea. Ethiopian nomads even rolled beans with animal fat to fashion a sort of traveler's quick-energy bar.

Since its discovery in Arabia around the ninth century, coffee has become one of the world's most popular agricultural products. In volume of trade, coffee is second only to oil on the world market. It is also one of the most labor-intensive food products, undergoing more than 17 processing steps on the way to the mugs of its followers.

The annual yield of a coffee tree is approximately one pound of roasted coffee or—brewed properly—about 40 cupfuls. It's a good thing this harvest is worth the wait, because coffee farmers have to do just that; on average, five years must pass before a young tree bears its first full harvest.

Arabica and Robusta

There are two major species of coffee that are grown for commercial use, *Coffea robusta* and *Coffea arabica*. Robusta grows at lower elevations, has a higher yield per plant, and is more disease resistant than its arabica relative. Robusta beans are noteworthy for their harsh, dirty flavor and abundant caffeine—twice as much caffeine, in fact, as is found in arabica beans. A relatively low cost of production make robustas a favorite with North American canned, or "institutional," coffee roasters.

The arabica species, which grows best at higher elevations, is the source of all of the world's great coffees. While there is more poor-tasting arabica than robusta in the world, this is simply a result of the fact that monumentally more arabica is grown. About 75 percent of the world's total production is arabica; at most, 10 percent of that is actually of "specialty" quality.

"SPECIALTY" QUALITY COFFEE

Specialty coffee distinguishes itself first and foremost by the quality of the raw material. The term "specialty coffee" also connotes a greater level of attention paid to the processing and roasting than is characteristically associated with coffee that comes in a can. Henceforth, when we talk about growing conditions and coffee in general, the specialty-grade arabicas are the beans we're talking about.

To narrow the pot still further, of the 10 percent of arabicas that can legitimately be called specialty coffee, only 1 or 2 percent qualify as superlative representatives of their growing regions, or *grand crus* ("great growths"). Such beans provide the pinnacle flavors and aromas we coffee lovers are looking for, and when we talk about taste in the cup, these are the coffees to which we refer. The stunning reward of a balance of factors including plant pedigree, altitude, microclimate, and cultivation, these magnificent coffees are the ones we encourage you to seek out and sample.

Here's a quick semantic distinction you may find useful: People often refer to single-origin coffees, the pure, unblended coffees that come from a single country or region, as "varietals." Used this way, the term is more colloquial and convenient than botanically correct.

Remember the hierarchy from high school biology—kingdom, phylum, class, and so on? "Species" falls at the end of the line, and "variety" is a subunit of species.

The use of the word varietal, therefore, is a bit misleading. When people say "varietal," they're not talking about a distinct "variety" within species *arabica;* what they really mean is a single-origin coffee. To avoid confusion, whenever we refer to unblended beans we will call them single-origin coffees.

HYBRIDS VS. HEIRLOOMS

As is the case with many domesticated agricultural products today, the issue of growing heirloom varieties versus modern hybrids is a great concern in the specialty coffee industry. Older versions of the arabica plant are preferred by many specialty coffee buyers for their superior and distinctive taste qualities. Older heirloom types, such as *bourbon* and *typica,* are still widely planted in East Africa, Yemen, Guatemala, and El Salvador. Significant pockets can be found in other countries as well.

At the same time, modern hybrids such as *caturra, catimor,* and the hardy *variedad Colombiana* have become increasingly popular with growers. In general, hybrids produce more beans per plant and are less susceptible to disease than the heirloom types. Unfortunately, hybrids are also generally considered by tasters in the industry to be more bland in the cup.

Specialty coffee buyers concerned about flavor and the future existence of fine coffee encourage growers to continue cultivating heirloom plants. They are also willing to pay the higher prices that support growers in doing so.

Photo ©1994 by Elizabeth Mangelsdorf

◆ ─────────────────────────────────────── ◆

Specialty coffee distinguishes itself first and foremost
by the quality of the raw material.

5

A seasoned picker in Guatemala's Antigua region pours coffee cherries over her head to sift out twigs and other debris.

Growing and Harvesting

The coffee tree requires a frost-free climate, moderate rainfall, and plenty of sunshine. The regions where coffee grows, known as "origin regions," are grouped loosely under three geographical nameplates: the Americas, Africa and Arabia, and Indonesia. Within these regions, coffee grows in almost 80 different countries. It can grow at altitudes ranging from sea level to 6,000 feet, in all sorts of different soils and microclimates.

The environment required for growing fine specialty coffee, however, is found only in select mountainous regions in the tropics—between the Tropic of Capricorn and the Tropic of Cancer, to be exact. These aristocrats demand high altitudes, usually between 4,000 and 6,000 feet, to produce their stunning and concentrated flavors. They need an annual rainfall of about 80 inches, with distinct rainy and dry seasons. The soil in which fine coffees grow must be extremely fertile, and is often volcanic. Regular mist and cloud cover are also necessary for protection from overexposure to sunlight at these latitudes.

For such high-quality coffee to thrive, year-round daytime temperatures must average 60–70°F, which by tropical standards is quite cool. The result is a longer, slower growth cycle, yielding beans that are denser and far more intense in flavor than their lower-grown neighbors. In some growing regions, most notably Guatemala and Costa Rica, beans are graded by elevation. The highest-grown of these are called "strictly hard bean" (SHB). In origin countries, you might also hear high-grown coffees described as being "stronger" (in taste, mind you—not caffeine content).

Because they are harder and more dense, high-grown beans can be roasted darker and still retain their integrity. Here's an example: At a darker roast, a premium Guatemalan Antigua offers plush, Belgian-chocolate body and considerable flavor complexity. At the same roast, beans grown at lower elevations are left with little other than the roasty, smokey flavors of the roasting process itself.

The beans grown downslope are still good coffee, but compared in the cup to those of higher elevations they are simple, mild, and uncomplicated. To borrow a winetaster's term, they are *vin ordinaire,* "ordinary wine," and nothing to write home about. Again, for true complexity and dimensionality of flavor, green-coffee buyers look to the lofty mountains, bright sunshine, fertile soil, and warm but not hot climes—the land, as the people of Guatemala call their highlands, of "eternal spring."

In addition to meeting these narrowly defined growing criteria, fine coffee requires special handling during its harvest. Coffee cherries ripen at differing rates—even on the same tree and branch, and in the same cluster. To ensure optimal flavor, cherries must be picked at their respective peaks. Each cherry is picked individually, by hand. Coffee pickers return many times to the same tree over the course of a harvest, and pick through each day's efforts with care in order to spot and discard any underripe fruit.

Wet and Dry Processing

After the ripe cherries have been plucked from their trees, the next task is to get at the seeds, or coffee beans, inside. To separate the beans from their cherries, a total of four layers

Anatomy of the Coffee Cherry

Coffee Branch with Cherries and Blossoms

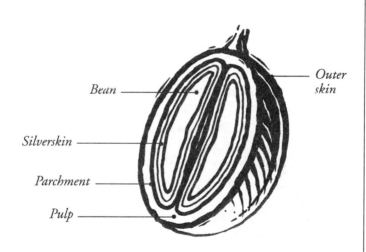

Bean —

Silverskin —

Parchment —

Pulp —

Outer
skin

Cross-section of a Coffee Cherry

Photo ©1994 by Elizabeth Mangelsdorf

After wet processing, coffee (with the parchment layer still on) is left to dry on large patios and must be raked several times each day.

must be removed: the tough, shiny outer skin; the sticky, mucilaginous pulp of the fruit; a stiff parchment casing; and the thin, delicate "silverskin" that clings to each bean.

There are two methods used to isolate the beans: the washed process and the dry process. The method used depends largely on the availability of fresh water and is one of the most important determinants of coffee flavor.

The washed, or wet, method involves mechanically removing the pulp from the beans. After depulping, top-quality wet-processed coffees are transferred to large fermentation tanks, usually through a sluice of some kind.

In the fermentation tanks, a carefully monitored and controlled enzymatic reaction allows the sticky fruit to swell and loosen from the beans inside. Many first-time plantation visitors are surprised to discover that these tanks of coffee smell remarkably like new-made wine. Fermentation may last from 12 to 36 hours, depending on atmospheric conditions and the nature of the coffee itself. Carefully executed, fermentation yields the crisp, fruity acidity and aromatic high notes that define the world's great washed coffees.

The path from ripe to rotten is short. If this stage is not arrested at the exact moment fermentation is complete, an entire batch of coffee can be ruined. The dreaded taste defect known as "ferment" will occur and lend its unmistakably offensive taste to the beans. When ferment is present, even a neophyte taster knows something has gone horribly wrong; its taste could be described, quite frankly, as latrine-like. The control of fermentation is invariably the job of the most experienced workers on a coffee plantation.

When fermentation is complete, the beans are washed free from the loosened fruit. The coffee beans, with parchment layer intact, are left to dry on large patios. To ensure even drying, the beans must be raked and thereby turned several times each day.

Washed coffees are brighter and offer cleaner, more consistent flavors than those processed by the dry method. Not surprisingly, the wet method predominates in Latin America, the very region whose coffees we associate with these characteristics. In more industrialized coffee-growing countries like Costa Rica, traditional wet processing is being replaced with a variation called aqua-pulping. With this method, the coffee is just depulped, rinsed, and dried. Sadly, such coffee can't express the high notes and varietal charm characteristic of traditionally washed beans.

In comparison to the wet method, the dry or natural method seems quite simple. Coffee cherries are spread to dry in open sunlight, usually on patios or tarps, for several weeks. The shriveled husks of dried fruit are then winnowed away, leaving only the interior parchment and beans.

Dry-processed coffees are generally heavier bodied and more variable in flavor than wet-processed beans. You will find—and learn to taste—that most Indonesian coffees are dry-processed, as are some of the more traditional coffees of Africa and Arabia.

Milling and Sorting

After being processed via the wet or dry method, coffee beans are milled to remove their stiff parchment and light, translucent silverskin. They are then sorted by size and density. At every step of the way, in fact, the milling and sorting processes work to bring like beans together, and this is critically important to good roasting. Defects, which may include broken or underripe beans and small stones, twigs, or other foreign material, are also removed during milling and sorting.

Separated from defects and shed of their trappings, coffee beans are known to the trade as "green coffee." In truth, unadulterated "green" beans range in color from opalescent blue to a matte gray-green. Compared to roasted coffee, which has a shelf life that is measured in days, green coffee is fairly stable, with a shelf life of up to one year.

From There to Here

How long does it take coffee to get from "picking point," or harvest, to the roaster? For properly selected coffee, it takes a while. The stretch of time between the moment coffee is harvested and the day it is received by the roaster is typically a minimum of two to three months. The prime picking point in Central America, for example, is January through March; the better Central American coffees harvested in March will begin reaching U.S. roasters in June and July.

Savvy green-coffee buyers avoid first shipments from any origin. These tend to comprise early pickings—less flavorful coffee that's been rushed to market. While top-quality Costa Rican coffees may be shipped as early as February, the best usually go out in April or May. These start arriving in U.S. ports by mid-summer.

Why does it take so long for green coffee to reach us? As you know, once harvested, the coffee will be wet-processed or dry-processed. It will be milled and sorted, then carefully dried to within 10 to 12 percent moisture, rendering it chemically stable. The sum of these processes can take up to 14 days. At the finest farms, the coffee will then sit in what is called *reposo,* or "rest," for 30 to 60 days. Much like the cask conditioning of beer and wine, the function of reposo is to allow coffee to settle down, to reach equilibrium with regard to its temperature and humidity. This step greatly extends its useful shelf life in green form which, again, is of substantial benefit to the roaster.

Following these days of rest, the coffee is transported by sea to its destination country. Travel from Central America to the United States may occupy the better part of a month. For coffees that start out further away, such as in Kenya or Papua New Guinea, the trip may take up to twice as long, or two full months.

A Brief History of the Bean

The history of the coffee bean does not want for drama. Since its first documented use—and probably long before—stories involving coffee have been rife with intrigue, passion, revolution, and idiosyncratic charm.

Of Goats and Holy Men

Legend has it that the stimulant properties of coffee were discovered sometime before the ninth century by an Abyssinian goatherd named Kaldi. Bored and mischievous, the young man's goats began snacking on coffee cherries while he napped nearby. Waking to find his charges pirouetting off rocks and the surrounding canyon walls, Kaldi collected a handful of the bright red fruit and hastened home to his village *imam*. As an experiment, the religious leader boiled the cherries in water and then drank the concoction himself. He became alert and lively, so much so that maintaining wakefulness during evening prayers was uncharacteristically effortless. These stimulating properties made coffee an instant hit among the ranks of the faithful, and its use rapidly became routine.

As coffee gained in popularity, the sixteenth-century Mohammeddans found reason to complain. Ironically, they considered coffee to be a threat to religious sobriety, especially upon witnessing that followers were more likely to frequent streetside cafés than they were to visit the mosques. Consumption was discouraged, and rumors linking the beverage with impotence, among other "ills," spread wildly. Still, there was no scarcity of coffee drinkers.

In fact, the Arabians guarded their beans with extreme jealousy. All coffee beans designated for export were boiled, destroying their ability to germinate and be domesticated outside the region. Although there is unofficial record that one religious pilgrim smuggled a seedling back to India in the early 1600s and planted it behind his hut in the Mysore area (where a great deal of good coffee has grown since), the commercial production of coffee remained under Arab control through the latter part of the century.

The Baptism of the Bean

Not long after Venetian traders first presented coffee to Europe in 1615, Pope Clement VIII was warned it might prove threatening to the holy aims of the Church. A legislature of priests accused the beverage of being a tool for the devil, designed to lure good worshippers into losing their souls. Curious, the pope requested that his attendants bring a cup of the stuff to him. He found its aroma pleasing and, upon tasting it, became so enamored with the brew that he decided to get the better of the devil by baptizing it, thereby making coffee a "truly Christian beverage."

The ardently entrepreneurial Dutch orchestrated the first successful planting outside Arabia—on the island of Java—in 1699. An initial trial shipment was sent back to Amsterdam in 1706 and included one seedling, which was planted in the botanical gardens. This tiny plant later played the role of parent seedling to the majority of the coffee grown in the western world.

When coffee so gained in popularity in Germany that it replaced other breakfast beverages, the eighteenth-century ruler Frederick the Great issued a desperate manifesto. "It is disgusting to notice the increase in the quantity of coffee used by my subjects," he declared, complaining with particular bitterness that the revenues for coffee went to foreign hands while profit from beer came to the crown. "My people," he protested, "must drink beer." Johann Sebastian Bach's famous one-act operetta, the *Coffee Cantata,* was a thinly veiled operatic criticism of the extraordinary lengths the royalty and upper classes took to keep common folk from enjoying the beverage.

The fashionable populations of Vienna and London willingly blessed the beverage as well, although it was a Turkish ambassador's introduction of coffee to Paris that sparked a veritable explosion of coffee culture. It was rumored that Louis XV spent $15,000 per year on coffee for his daughters. Even the most avid coffee drinkers are astonished to hear that Voltaire supposedly consumed 50 cups a day. Balzac, another devotee among the French literati, applied its exciting properties thusly: He went to bed at six in the evening, slept until midnight, then rose for 12 solid hours of writing, during which time his sole sustenance was coffee.

Coffee Crosses the Atlantic

After numerous disappointing attempts, a coffee seedling measuring about five feet tall was successfully transplanted from the botanical gardens in Amsterdam to the gardens in Paris. Soon after, a young naval officer, Gabriel Mathieu de Clieu, triumphed as a coffee pioneer by bringing one of the plant's offspring to the Americas.

According to his own account, De Clieu shared his shipboard water ration with the plant, fended off jealous shipmates, and survived both storm and calm to finally triumph in planting the little tree when he docked at Martinique. Within 50 years, there were more than 18 million coffee trees growing on the island; these were the progenitors of most of the coffee plants growing in Central and South America today.

Consumption of coffee in the United States began as early as 1668. The first documented license to sell coffee was obtained by Dorothy Jones of the Massachusetts Colony in 1670. It was the famous British tax on tea, however, that elevated the role of coffee forever. The British East India Tea Company harbored plans to develop a profitable market in the colonies. But the Boston Tea Party, plotted by revolutionaries in Boston's lively Green Dragon coffee house, made drinking coffee a popular form of protest against the iron fist of the monarchy. From that point forward, the more refined beverage of the British crown never regained a substantial foothold.

Today, the United States consumes more coffee than any other nation in the world. Although per capita intake peaked in the 1960s, our national average is again on the rise. Numbers indicate that the fuel behind this, and a parallel increase in Canada, is the emerging specialty coffee segment of the market. Clearly, an emphasis on better coffee is attracting consumers back to it.

The Name Game: Reading Coffee Labels

There is an abundance of information that could be placed on a coffee bag or store menuboard. The level of detail varies from roaster to roaster and retailer to retailer, for a variety of reasons. Ultimately, the information passed along to the consumer can range from frustratingly minimal to exhaustingly overbearing.

Blend, Dark Roast, or Single-Origin?

At the very least, the name you find on the bag or label of a given coffee will tell you if the beans constitute a blend, a dark roast, or a single-origin coffee. Each of these is discussed in depth in subsequent chapters, but the most important thing to understand at this stage is how they differ from one another.

BLENDS

A blend is a combination of coffees from different countries. Blend names, while often fanciful, usually provide an indication of the character of the blend or the circumstances under which it is designed to be enjoyed. On a menu board, they aren't hard to spot: Except in some rare cases, the word "blend" will appear.

Many consumers assume that all coffees are blends, but this is not the case. Over 80 percent of all coffees offered are single-origin coffees, or beans from one specific country. These are combined in blends for all sorts of reasons and, as blends, are highly individualized by the roasters who create them. What we want you to know is that while the blends are certainly out there, there are other options, too.

DARK ROASTS

Typically, the darker roasts are also easy to find. Most of them contain the word "roast" in their name. Dark roasts are confusing, however, because there are no standard terms for them within the coffee industry; one roaster's French roast is another's full city. Moreover, the bean or blend of beans to which a given roast is applied usually plays a vital role in determining flavor. This means neither the roast name nor the bean's color offers a reliable way to predict flavor. The only way around this is to learn the terminology and flavor characteristics offered by individual roasters.

That said, there are some general comments about dark roast names that can be made. Roasts at the lighter end of the dark range, most often referred to by terms such as "Vienna" or "full city," are characterized by medium-to-dark brown color and a glossy bloom of natural coffee oils that coats the beans. These are medium-dark roasts by international standards, but many roasters on the West Coast, including the industry leader, Starbucks Coffee Company, roast all of their coffees at least this dark. This roast style emphasizes body, relegating acidity and aroma to background roles.

The very darkest roast, which usually goes by a name such as Italian or French roast, is nearly jet black. At this dramatic roast, coffee is characterized by flavors that are not the result of its own nature but of the extreme degree to which it has been roasted.

Some roasters provide coffees at multiple degrees of roast. Here again, you will probably see a single-origin coffee with its roast name attached. The name might be part of a widely used but imperfectly applied continuum, as in the case of "Guatemala Full City." Or it may be a specific designation coined by the roaster herself, such as "Guatemala *al fine.*"

In any case, don't hesitate to inquire if attached terms are an indication of roast. Ask the salesperson to describe the degree and characteristics of the roast as applied to the specific coffee or blend. Pursuing the definition of *al fine,* for example, you will discover that it means "to the finish" in Italian. This knowledge alone provides an inkling as to what the roaster intends by using it—and consequently the approximate character of the tastes you can expect.

SINGLE-ORIGIN COFFEES

Finally—and these make up most of what you will see—there are single-origin coffees. As we mentioned earlier, the word often used to mean single-origin, "varietal," is a misnomer. It does roll right off the tip of the tongue; marketing people love it. But the more rigid truth is that all the world's fine coffees come from the same botanical varietal: *Coffea arabica*. The phrase "single-origin" is simply more accurate.

A single-origin offering is always the fruit of one particular country, but it may also represent a particular region within that country (Hawaiian Kona is an example). In many instances, the designation will be more precise: farm or estate name, often accompanied by information concerning the grade.

Grading, Estate Names, and So On

The norms—and names—used for describing single-origin coffees vary from country to country, and roasters have widely deviating views on how much information is appropriate to supply to the consumer. In most cases, you're likely to see less information than is actually available.

Many roasters of great integrity would label an offering simply "Costa Rica," knowing all the while that it is actually "Costa Rica Tres Rios La Magnolia '96–'97 crop." Why such severe editing? For one thing, consumers as a general rule aren't overly fond of change. Coffee drinkers seem to have a hard time embracing coffee as an agricultural product, and it makes them nervous to see regional names and subnames altered from one season to another. Consequently, when the roaster is making adjustments that ensure consistent quality, her customers become concerned. "What was wrong with the last Costa Rica?" they're prone to asking, or, "Is this one as good?"

The question of how coffees change from region to region and crop to crop is an intriguing one and certainly worthy of discussion. But the confusion inspired in most consumers by changes in presentation is hard on the roaster, and can be hard on business quite irrespective of the quality of the coffees. Certain levels of labeling specificity, therefore, are often abandoned. Learn how to read what you see, and don't be afraid to ask questions.

GRADING

Grading designations, which differ greatly from country to country, may also appear on coffee labels. Coffees are graded by size and density, (sometimes) by the altitude at which they are grown, and, most importantly, by the number of defects permitted per pound. Here are some examples.

In most of Central America, the better coffees are graded by the altitude at which they are grown. In Guatemala, for example, the top grade is strictly hard bean (SHB), which denotes a dense coffee that owes its heft and concentrated flavor to having been grown at or above the minimum SHB altitude of 1,600 meters (approximately 4,500 feet). Similarly, *altura*—which means "high" in Spanish—is a designation applied to Mexican coffees that come from higher elevations and therefore possess the potential for greater flavor.

In Colombia, the largest possible bean size is the *supremo,* which many wrongly assume means "supreme." Supremos command a slight premium over the smaller *excelso* grade, but do not necessarily offer better flavor. Large, evenly sized beans look impressive and roast more evenly, but size alone is not an indicator of cup quality.

"Defects" include obvious flaws such as sticks, stones, and insects, as well as more subtle ones like the presence of under- or overripe beans. The best coffees have virtually no defects, which allows the bright fruit flavors inherent in coffee to shine through unimpeded.

REGION, FARM, AND ESTATE NAMES

Specific green coffees are sold to roasters under names that vary just as widely as the sum total of what the consumer sees. The first level of geographical detail beyond the name of the country is apt to be the coffee's origin region. This is a designation that quite often reaches the consumer, especially at the hands of more conscientious roasters.

Ethiopian Sidamo, for example, comes from an extremely high plateau (about 8,000 feet) facing the Red Sea. Ethiopia Harrar comes from an area that lies farther south, near the border with Somalia. Coffees from Harrar are dry-processed, which informs their winy, berry-like character and good body. Sidamos, on the other hand, are wet-processed, which contributes to their almost perfume-like aromas and gossamer lightness. The separate regions and their corresponding methods of processing both help to create distinctly different flavor profiles. Region names, when they appear, can be a tip-off that tells you to expect these differences.

Growers who invest the extra effort required to produce top quality coffee are proud of what they yield, and understandably so. They often designate their very best coffees with some sort of proprietary name. The very finest coffees produced by the La Minita farm in the Tarrazu region of Costa Rica, for example, bear the name of the farm itself: "Costa Rica Tarrazu La Minita," or "Costa Rica La Minita." In countries where coffee is grown on smaller farms, such titled ownership is impossible. When this coffee is gathered from such smallholders and graded by exporters, however, the exporters themselves often create their own descriptive "marks" to designate pinnacle offerings.

For countries such as Kenya, where tiny quantities of top coffee must be culled from small farms, roasters may use designations like "estate" or "estate select" to designate a series of coffees being offered during one crop year. Each coffee in a given "estate" series comes from a specific farm or group of farms that share identical growing conditions.

The Broken Chain of Custody

At the retail level, the presence of an estate name on a coffee bag or bin may mean something—or nothing at all. It may mean that the roaster is dedicated to securing the highest quality raw material, and wants to pass along the specifics to give some credit to the farmer. But—and we will make this point many times because it is so critical to an understanding of good coffee—even the best green beans represent only the potential for great coffee. Rather than becoming fixed on any specific coffee, region, or estate, make sure and buy your coffee from a source who realizes that great coffee begins with great beans.

Remember that coffee beans are to the final cup what grapes are to a bottle of wine, and it is the bottle of wine consumers want to buy. There's never any guarantee that if you purchase Costa Rica La Minita, you will have a good experience. Even estate-grown coffees are really not like estate-bottled wine, because in no place in the world is coffee roasted and sold fresh from the hills where it was grown. This broken chain of custody, which stretches all the way to the cup, can cause problems. A great cup depends on a long line of intricately linked variables.

If you are a retailer or restaurateur who sells or serves coffee, we encourage you to educate your customers about the coffees they drink. Information will empower them to make pleasing choices; once intimidated, they may never darken your door again. Don't be afraid to let customers know what you know about your coffees. Knowledge increases the pleasure of the coffee experience and gives coffee lovers a mechanism for providing you with valuable, specific feedback.

A Taster's Guide to Cupping Coffees

Imagine starting your day with 40 cups of fresh-brewed coffee. Imagine tasting these coffees by the spoonful, one after the other, in rapid succession. Now imagine being able to tell them all apart.

Most professional coffee tasters start their days by "cupping," that is, tasting a long row of coffees. Each glass or thick, white porcelain cup contains a different coffee sample, often from the previous day's roasting. The coffees are arranged in order of taste, with the lighter, brighter coffees first and the heavier, murkier ones down the line. Unlike a wine taster's domain, there is no cozy banter in the cupping room. The room itself is typically sparse and medical-looking; conversation is efficient and brusque.

At the cupping table, there are no price tags and no glossy marketing brochures. There is simply coffee: aroma, acidity, body, and flavor. Contrary to popular perception, competent tasting has little to do with inherited skill. Instead, expertise grows from regular, consistent exposure. Familiarity and concentration lead to the development of a library of taste memories that the cupper uses as reference points. Tasters can tell the difference between brews and with practice, so can you.

While tasting a series of coffees at the same time is a commonplace experience for professionals, it is often a revelation for consumers. Instead of falling in love exclusively with the first good coffee you find, routine tasting allows you to see how different coffees taste relative to one another. With practice, you can cultivate an understanding of the roles green-coffee type, roast degree, and freshness play in determining flavor. As you gain more experience, the ability to relate descriptions of coffee flavors with your tastings will help you to identify and locate the coffees you prefer.

Please don't feel bound to the tasting terms we present here. While there are ways to categorize and describe coffees objectively, the actual experience of coffee will always be subjective. Feel free to borrow adjectives from other areas of your life and experience—the most effective descriptions always do. Describing taste sensations is not unlike poetry in both process and result: Sip, and be inspired.

The Cupping Procedure

The cupping procedure is simple, direct, and virtually identical throughout the coffee trade. In preparation for a tasting, a standard measure of coffee (two tablespoons) is ground finely and placed in each tasting cup. Each cup is then filled with filtered, just-off-the-boil water. For the next few minutes, the job of the taster is simply to wait.

The official tasting process is initiated with the "breaking of the crust," or the puncturing of the tight cap of grounds that have risen to the surface. The taster uses a spoon to stir these grounds, leaning close to inhale the coffee's aroma as it is released. To avoid singeing any taste buds, the infusion is allowed to cool slightly. As it cools, the coffee grounds settle on the bottom of the cup. (If you slurp prematurely, get ready to chew. It normally takes an additional three to five minutes for the grounds to sink.)

Using a soup spoon, the taster slurps the coffee loudly. This aerates the coffee, coating the taster's entire mouth; even coating is crucial to a complete experience of what each coffee has to offer. After slurping, the taster spits out the coffee in order to avoid excessive stimulation from its ready amounts of caffeine.

Experienced tasters taste each coffee at least twice: once near normal drinking temperature and again when the coffee is tepid. At higher temperatures, one perceives primarily the body, or weight and viscosity, of the coffee. As the liquid cools, subtleties of aroma, acidity, and varietal flavor show through more clearly. This is why all scalding hot coffees taste pretty much the same—and why our most positive taste memories of coffee are based on that last, lingering sip.

The first concern of professional cuppers is to detect taints or defects. Theoretically, buyers of specialty grades should be able to assume the quality is high enough that any sample they receive will be without flavor defects. This is, unfortunately, not the case. Even more regrettable is the fact that many smaller roasters depend not on their palates but on green-coffee importers to execute quality control on their behalf. These roasters are taking quite a risk, expecting the importer to weed out the coffees it is his very job to sell.

Talking about Taste

When tasting coffee, the two most important tools you can use are your mouth and your nose. The key to talking successfully about tasting is to learn to describe what they encounter during the tasting process.

Key flavors are sensed on different areas of the tongue. Acidity and sweetness, which are both critically important to recognize when cupping coffee, are tasted primarily on the tip of the tongue. Sourness and saltiness are perceived most strongly on the sides. Bitterness is gauged predominantly at the back, while body (the "weight" of the brew, measured by using your tongue like a scale) registers across the entire surface.

Smell makes up a significant part of what you "taste." During tasting, you use your mouth not only to sense key flavors but also as a vehicle for accessing the olfactory cavity. Molecules drift up from your mouth into the nasal cavity, and from there to the olfactory cavity and bulbs. The olfactory bulbs are your sense organs for smell. With the aid of these organs, you can distinguish between 2,000 and 4,000 different aromas.

When they describe coffees, tasters do so in terms of three basic categories of sensation: acidity, body, and flavor. Understanding these terms helps the beginning taster understand and articulate taste sensations, and make sense of the lush descriptions on coffee bins.

How to Cup Coffee at Home

The best ways to brew coffee are usually the most straightforward, and this is one of them. Brewing coffee for a cupping is a bit like preparing "cowboy coffee" in the bottom of a kettle—except that you will want to prepare it in individual cups and pay much more attention to the brewing than is typical for that method!

As an approximate alternative to the standard cupping protocol, you can use coffee press pots for brewing. Chapter 7, "Brewing Great Coffee at Home," provides detailed instructions.

Materials

- Six-ounce cups, preferably porcelain or glass (1 cup per coffee being tasted per taster)

- One soup spoon per taster

- One rinsing container (an auxiliary cup of water or a nearby sink)

- A convenient place to spit coffee (the sink or an extra cup, bowl, or container)

- One quart of cold, fresh water

- Coffee: one standard coffee measure (2 tablespoons) per type of coffee per taster

Instructions

1. Grind your beans to a consistency akin to the coarseness of cornmeal (and like that used for professional, or "flat-bottom filter," drip coffee). NOTE: As we emphasize elsewhere, the use of fresh coffee—and therefore the use of a grinder—is one of the most critical elements to creating a superlative coffee experience. If you do not want to

invest in a small blade grinder, be aware that you are sacrificing a great deal of flavor.

2. For each coffee being tasted, place 1 standard measure of ground coffee in the bottom of a cup for each taster. (In the tasting room, coffee is weighed because different coffees are of differing densities. If you use a scale, measure out 10 grams of whole-bean coffee for each cup, then grind it.)

3. Boil your water. Your water should be clear of foreign tastes and contaminants, and fresh. When the water has reached a boil, take it off the burner and wait for a split second to achieve the optimal just-off-boil contact temperature.

4. Fill each cup with hot water. Do this in the same order you plan to taste the coffees to ensure proper brewing time. Leave a little room at the top of each cup, perhaps 1/8 inch.

5. Wait two minutes, then break the crust. The carbon dioxide released from your beautiful, freshly ground coffee will have caused the grounds to swell into a granular, dry-looking arch. Bring your nose down close to the cup, and use the gentle edge of your spoon to break into the swollen grounds. This provides a full first impression of the coffee's aroma and is of paramount importance to the cupping ritual. Enjoy it. Remember to rinse your spoon between cups.

6. Allow the grounds to settle. When the coffees are cool enough to taste, and all the grounds have

settled to the bottom (this normally takes about 3 to 5 minutes), take your spoon in hand again. Dip it into the coffee, and…

7. *Slurp.* Remember that you want to coat your mouth evenly with the coffee. This may take some practice. With each slurp, you are aerating the coffee and therefore releasing more aroma to your olfactory bulbs (the sense organs for smell, located just above your nasal cavity). Pretend you're drinking through a straw—precisely what your mother always taught you not to do at the table.

Recording Your Experience

We suggest keeping paper and pencil handy during a tasting, enough for everyone who participates. It is best to write your impressions down while they seem indelible (because they aren't). The very process of writing will help you recall the experience of individual coffees. It also encourages the beginning taster to conjure adjectives and discuss the experience, which is what it's all about—and which they otherwise might feel too shy to initiate.

Try writing at two separate junctures: about aroma at the breaking of the crust, and about your impressions of the coffee's acidity, body, and flavor after slurping. Take several slurps, to clear impressions of the previous sample and gain a good feel for the coffee in question. Taste each coffee at varying stages of cooling, and note the specifics of their transitions.

ACIDITY

This tasting term is one of the most important—and misunderstood. Most people relate acidity with objective pH level; they think of grapefruit juice or the associated stomach upset. But all coffees are low in *this* sort of acidity.

The word acidity, as it pertains to coffee tasting, is a positive term that denotes sparkling crispness, a vibrant burst of winy, palate-cleansing fruit. Bright, nuanced acidity is what high-grown washed coffees are all about.

Acidity is often confused with bitterness, lending to the fact that the word "bitter" is used somewhat indiscriminately. True bitterness in coffee is the result of two things: (1) overextraction, which is caused by running too much water through too little coffee; and (2) dark roasting, which creates an intentional roasty darkness that some coffee drinkers enjoy as they do similar characteristics in a bitter aperitif or Scotch whiskey. A very small—and generally undetectable—amount of bitterness also comes from the presence of caffeine.

BODY

Body refers to an experience of weight, the feel of the coffee on one's tongue. A coffee's body can range from light to medium to full—or even buttery or syrupy—and varies with origin region (Latin Americans are generally light- to medium-bodied, while Indonesians such as Sumatra are typically the fullest in body) and brewing method. Plunger pots and espresso machines produce far heavier body than drip brewers. Paper filters remove oils, so conventional drip coffee is lighter in body than coffee brewed paper-free.

FLAVOR

Flavor refers to the taster's total impression of aroma, acidity, and body. The term is used in a general sense to indicate intensity ("this coffee is flavorful") and to acknowledge specific characteristics such as spice, fruit, and chocolate notes.

With these three categories as a framework, coffee can be described with a vocabulary as passionate and varied as a poet's. A Sulawesi might be said to have "enormously full body; complex herbal, earthy flavors; and a creamy butter-caramel finish." In the cup, a fine Ethiopian Yergacheffe may be "light-bodied and lively, with a strikingly intense, perfumed bouquet of ripe peaches and apricots." The same Yergacheffe, continues the cupper, boasts "honeyed sweetness and a lemon-peel acidity."

Whatever you do, don't feel intimidated by the language. Not unlike wine tasting terms, the standard vocabulary used to describe coffees is designed to communicate specific impressions of taste and aroma. There is a glossary with a number of the more common terms and their definitions in Appendix A, and we encourage you to add new words to the list!

Enjoying coffee is about being in touch with taste. To help you get started, we have included several suggested tastings on the pages that follow. These tastings are designed to acquaint you with each of the three origin regions—what the regions' coffees share in common, as well as the diversity that exists among them. Now it's your turn: Slurp, savor, and say it in your own words.

Suggested Coffee Tastings

As you begin to branch out with your own "theme" tastings, we suggest comparing coffees from different regions, and tasting blends alongside their component coffees. In all cases, arrange your tastings with body in mind, always progressing from lightest to heaviest on the first pass.

Latin America and the Pacific

Coffees: *Brazil, Kona, Colombia, Costa Rica Tarrazu.* In a sense, this combination enables you to "taste your way up the mountain." The progression moves from mild to intense, simple to complex, and murky to crystal clear.

The bland, nutty flavor of a good Brazil connects with most people's earliest memories of coffee drinking, since Brazils are the dominant component of most mass-market blends. This is the taste of low-altitude, dry-processed coffee. A good Kona will be simple and straightforward, with the slight acidity and flavors characteristic of low-grown washed arabicas. The Colombian will be fuller-bodied, with somewhat greater acidity. The Costa Rican, finally, will offer pointed acidity and clear, multidimensional flavors.

East Africa and Arabia

Coffees: *Ethiopian Yergacheffe* or *Sidamo, Kenya Estate, Yemen Mocha Sanani* or *Mattari.* Step backward in time; this combination presents two washed coffees and one natural (dry-processed) that together may well comprise the original taste of coffee. Preeminent washed coffees are juxtaposed against the natural, uncovering fruit versus earthy funk.

The Yergacheffe (especially at a relatively light roast) will exert a powerful, almost perfumed aroma, light body, and exotic acidity. Kenya, by comparison, expresses itself as a brooding heavyweight; these beans combine heavy body and powerful, dark fruit acidity in much the same way a fine red wine does. The Yemen is the ultimate in complexity. It offers wildness and idiosyncrasy, notes of blueberry, cocoa, wood, and spice, and a lingering aftertaste.

Indonesia

Coffees: *Papua New Guinea, Estate Java, Sumatra, Sulawesi.* The New Guinea comes across more like a Latin American coffee—but on a grand scale. It offers abundant, fruity acidity and medium to heavy body. The Java is an experience of pure body, with flavors that may remind you of freshly roasted nuts and an almost olive oil-style viscosity. Because of their washed flavor characteristics, these coffees are exceptions to the regional rule.

A good Sumatra, on the other hand, will coat the palate with incredibly heavy body and the dense flavors of herb and earth. It bypasses the tip of the tongue, where acidity and sweetness are perceived, almost altogether. Sulawesi adds forest-floor-type flavors, such as mushroom and moss, in concert with a butter caramel sweetness that contrasts broadly with the dry style of the Sumatra.

C H A P T E R   5

Regional Character

Visit the cellar of a great wine maker and you are certain to find a library of previous vintages. The vintner himself is the foremost expert regarding the flavor of his wine. In all likelihood, he knows not only how his product rates relative to the fruits of close neighbors, but also how his wine compares to other wines made from similar grapes around the world.

Visit an equally prestigious farm in a great coffee-growing region like Antigua, Guatemala, and you will probably be served a cup of bad instant coffee. In fact, few coffee farmers anywhere have even tasted the coffee they grow. The handful that have lack exposure to other coffees and so don't know how theirs compare. Coffee is a cash crop in most countries where it is grown; the best beans are exported, and only the lesser grades are reserved for domestic consumption.

A Taste of Place: Finding the Great Coffees

Historically, growers have focused on the health of their plants, the integrity of processing, and how the final products *look*. This orientation, while important and admirable, is not directly useful to the roasters and green-coffee buyers who make choices based on *taste*. Increasing interest in specialty coffee and rapidly expanding global communication networks are beginning to bridge the chasm between growing coffee and understanding its resultant flavors. Nevertheless, it is still important to understand the discrepancy to appreciate the critical role that professional tasters—including exporters, importers, and particularly roasters—play in ferreting out great coffees.

THE "GRAND CRUS"

In France, the greatest wines from the best vineyards and vintages are greatly revered. They are set aside for celebratory consumption on the most special of occasions. Undoubtedly a question of expense, this habit is also a practical one. The great wines are massive, powerful, multidimensional experiences that tend to upstage food. They are often best appreciated by themselves.

The *grand crus,* or "great growths," of the coffee world are few in number and similarly demanding. Each conveys a unique "taste of place," a compelling flavor window into the singular growing conditions of its homeland. Powerful and dynamic, the grand crus require a certain vigilant enjoyment on the part of the coffee drinker.

They are the best beans, but not appropriate for every use. It would be a waste of money, for example, to sizzle

Rating Scale for Single-Origin Coffees

◆━━◆

The components and sequence of this list may surprise you: Some of the more familiar coffees fall at the bottom! Without apology, and in the name of seizing this opportunity to emphasize the world's greats, our goal is to take you along the most direct route to them. Detailed discussions of each coffee are presented on the following pages. (NOTE: This ranking is based on current performance.)

Key: * * * * *   = outstanding   * * *   = average
            * * * *   = very good   * *   = mediocre

LATIN AMERICA AND THE PACIFIC

Guatemalan Antigua (genuine, from selected estates)	***/*****
Costa Rican Dota	*****
Costa Rican La Minita	*****
Top regional Guatemalan SHB estate coffees	***/*****
Estate-grown Costa Rican Tres Rios and Tarrazu	***/****
Panama Estate	***/****
Salvadoran (estate coffees)	***/*****
Colombian (from premier regions)	**/****
Mexican Altura (from top farms)	**/****
Kona	**/***
Caribbean specialties: Jamaican, Haitian, Dominican	**
Brazilian fancy grades	**

EAST AFRICA AND ARABIA

Kenya AA (estate-grown auction lots from main crop)	*****
Ethiopian Yergacheffe and Sidamo (carefully selected lots)	***/*****
Yemen Mocha Sanani and Mattari	***/*****
"Generic" Kenya AA	***
Zimbabwe (from top estates)	***/****
Malawi (from top estates)	**/****
Ethiopian Harrar	**/****
Ethiopian Limu	**/***
Ethiopian Djimmah, Ghimbi	**/***

INDONESIA

Sumatra Mandheling (Grade 1, special preparation)	****/*****
Sulawesi (top grades)	****/*****
Papua New Guinea (from top estates)	****/*****
Java Estate	***/****
Java (nonestate and "private" estate)	**
Aged Indonesians (Sumatra, Sulawesi)	**/*****

superior beans in a French roast or to blunt their complex flavors with large quantities of milk or flavorings.

Happily, the greats of the coffee world—unlike their vinous counterparts—are affordable luxuries: Even at $13 per pound, each serving provides unbeatable value at about 32 cents. That said, remember that there is no linear relationship between price and quality. Many highly touted and expensive coffees are only mediocre in the cup.

IDENTIFYING THE TASTES THAT PLEASE YOU

The coffee evaluations in this chapter are based solely on cup quality, and are designed to help you navigate the dense forest of origin countries, grading designations, and estate names to find the tastes that please you most. The task that now lies before you, should you choose to accept it, is to *taste*—because the only way to become truly knowledgeable about coffees is to sample them widely.

There is no way to predict what tastes you will gravitate toward initially, or what offerings you will choose over time. Experience with good coffees is a spiraling of epiphanies. Adventuresome eaters, and those who already invest great time and energy in seeking out and preparing other specialty foods, tend to have a high tolerance for daring amounts of acidity, of both the fruit and tannic variety.

Those who are more "comfort food" oriented usually start with a beverage with which they can relax: milk-based drinks and muted, heavy-bodied coffees. For relative newcomers to coffee, the mild and accessible Latin Americans are the most approachable bridge into specialty coffee flavors. And at some degree of roast, a good Kenya will make everybody happy!

While most of the work that goes into a cup of coffee does happen on the farm, even great green beans don't guarantee great taste. Coffee grown beautifully, processed perfectly, and roasted impeccably can still fall to ruin before it reaches the cup. Guard your coffee's freshness with care, build your brewing skills, be consistent. And experiment.

WHERE TO BUY GOOD COFFEE

Depending on where you live, a consistent source of good coffee may be just down the street or hundreds of miles away. The best coffees come from companies that employ one or more seasoned, expert tasters—and that can afford to compete for and stock green coffees that are rare and costly. Oddly, both large national companies and the smallest "microroasters" have difficulty meeting these criteria.

Such microroasters are often coffee industry newcomers and thus lack the tasting expertise and financial resources required to source and maintain an inventory of top quality green coffees. Such firms may also fall short of the roasting sophistication and quality control standards offered by the best larger roasters. That said, many small roasters we know are passionate about what they do, and are committed to offering the freshest possible coffee.

The guidelines for taste profiles, coffee freshness, and brewing that we provide over the next few chapters will help you evaluate the different coffee sources available. And no matter from whom you ultimately buy your coffee, you may want to start with the consistent flavors and expert information provided by more established roasters. For many coffee lovers, these serve as a good starting point and a solid frame of reference for exploration.

Rating Your Coffee Retailer

Many—but unfortunately not all—retailers are committed to offering their customers an excellent selection of fresh-roasted coffees. You may want to keep the following guidelines in mind as a way to "rate" the quality of the coffee sources available to you.

Good Signs	Bad Signs
• Not more than a total of 30 coffees offered for sale.	• Offers an overly extensive inventory of roasted coffees (how can they all be fresh?).
• Staff can tell you when coffees were roasted, and ensures that beans in bins are sold within a week.	• Staff measures whole bean freshness in months, or doesn't know how freshness is monitored at all.
• A modest number of drip coffees are served (i.e., 2–3), and staff knows when they were brewed.	• 12 or more brewed coffees sit in airpots or (worse!) glass carafes, waiting…
• Carries *grand cru* coffees.	• Features costly coffees from Hawaii, Jamaica, and Puerto Rico.
• Offers no chemically flavored beans.	• Assertive odors of various flavored coffees compete for attention.
• Has a coffee-loving staff that is not afraid to offer information and answer questions.	• Features disinterested, "fast-food" type service.
• Serves superb, carefully made coffee drinks.	• Coffee beverages are mediocre (it is logical—and fair—to judge a store's bean quality by that of their beverages).

The Three Great Growing Regions: The Americas, Africa and Arabia, Indonesia

Over the pages that follow, we will walk through the three primary coffee-growing regions. By discussing specific regions, estate names, and other designations, we are seeking not only to present pertinent information, but to provide valuable clues that you can use to evaluate quality as you buy your own coffees. Again, please bear in mind that circumstances at individual farms and within origin countries change every crop year, making your roaster's ability to cup and select infinitely more important than the presence or absence of a particular name on the bean bag or menu board.

We start with the Americas, the lightest, brightest, and generally most accessible of the world's coffees. Next, we move to the Africans, successors of the earliest coffee trees and known for their wild, rustic flavors. The last region we discuss is that of the earthy, full-bodied Indonesians. Not coincidentally, this order loosely parallels a standard tasting progression; one should always move from the lightest to the heaviest when tasting multiple coffees.

THE AMERICAS

Central and South America together are responsible for providing the world with a significant amount of coffee. More impressive than the sheer quantities produced in this area, however, is the fact that in the minds of most North American consumers this region defines the taste of coffee altogether. As recently as 50 years ago, books on coffee devoted themselves primarily to the established growing

Regional Characteristics at a Glance

As a preview to the detailed coffee descriptions on the following pages, this chart provides brief flavor associations for the significant coffees of each growing region. Use these thumbnail sketches for ongoing reference, or to identify new coffees you want to try.

LATIN AMERICA AND THE PACIFIC

Coffee	Thumbnail Flavor Sketch
South America	
Brazil	Nutty, low-acid, simple to bland
Colombia	Heavy-bodied, rich, simple, and solid
Central America	
Guatemala	Dark chocolate with spice, smoke, fruit
Costa Rica	Tangy, consistent, sweet
Mexico	Light, nutty milk chocolate
Hawaii and the Caribbean	
Jamaica	Bland, neutral
Hawaii	Mild, sweet, neutral

EAST AFRICA AND ARABIA

Coffee	Thumbnail Flavor Sketch
Ethiopian Harrar	Winey, wild, blueberry-like
Ethiopian Yergacheffe/ Sidamo	Lemony, elegant, mentholated; intensely aromatic
Yemen Mocha	Fruit-like, musky, earthy, sweetly spicy, chocolatey, tobacco-like
Kenya	Bright, hearty, lush black-currant flavor

INDONESIA

Coffee	Thumbnail Flavor Sketch
Java	Hearty, peppery spice
Sumatra	Earthy, woodsy, smooth, herbal aroma
Sulawesi	Caramelly, buttery, sweet, syrupy
Papua New Guinea	Tropical fruit-like, pungent, clean, bright
Other	
India	Dark chocolate, nutmeg, clove spice

regions of Africa, Arabia, and Indonesia and presented only a few scattered comments on promising new plantings in countries with names like Colombia and Brazil.

Typically, consumers find the flavor profiles of Latin American coffees to be accessible and welcoming. High-grown, well-prepared coffees from this region have a familiar and reassuring quality to them. They taste, one might say, like transmuted versions of the canned coffee on which most of us were raised. The soft, balanced flavors we remember are there, but gone are the rubbery coarseness of robusta and the mealy, cereal-like staleness characteristic of coffee trapped in a can.

Our discussion of Latin American coffees also includes several "geographical fibbers." Although the island coffees of Hawaii and the Caribbean don't meet the strict geographical criteria, their flavors place them clearly within this category.

Brazil *(Dry-Processed)*

Brazil produces by far the largest quantity of coffee in the world. The vast majority of the country's yield is low-grown arabica, ranging in quality from extremely poor to passable. Brazilian coffee is the predominant flavor you taste in nearly every cup of run-of-the-mill American coffee: bland, woody, and innocuous.

The very nicest Brazils are nutty, low-acid coffees best suited for use in Italian-style espresso blends, where their mildness and lack of high notes are virtues. A tiny coterie of firms are currently working to produce more nuanced and complex Brazils from carefully selected microclimates. To date, the most promising efforts come from farms such as Fazenda Vista Allegre (F.V.A.) and Capim Branco. If you encounter them, these coffees are worth tasting; they offer a

more appealing rendition of the flavors most of us connect
with our earliest coffee memories.

Colombia *(Wet-Processed)*

Colombia stands alone among origin countries for the
outstanding job it has done in marketing itself. The
legendary figure of Juan Valdez® (who is not a real coffee
farmer, although he does play one on television) has
convinced legions of consumers that all Colombian coffee is
"specialty"—or at least very special—coffee.

In truth, the country has done an exceptional job of
producing huge quantities of good-quality coffee.
Colombia's emphasis on quantity and market share has
resulted in widely standardized production, yielding coffee
which, while it rarely sinks to great depths, is equally
unlikely to achieve great heights. Decent Colombian coffee
is easy to find. But stellar examples, the stuff romanced by
the descriptions in classic coffee books and today's slick ad
campaigns, are few and far between. For most retailers, this
isn't a major problem; the numbers prove that Colombian
sells regardless of how it actually tastes.

In contrast to the better plantation-grown coffees of
neighboring countries, which are processed by skilled
employees in fully equipped wet-processing *beneficios,*
Colombian coffee is both grown and processed by small
farmers. After processing, the coffee is bulked together for
dry milling and sale. As a result, most Colombian coffees are
combinations of beans whose initial quality varies widely.

In addition to the traditional, small-scale wet milling,
there are two reasons Colombian coffee cannot be ranked
among the greater Central Americans. The first is the
prevalence of a high-yield, inferior-tasting hybrid called

variedad Colombiana. Second, the bulk of Colombian coffee comes from areas where the altitude, latitude, and microclimate are less than ideal.

In a blind tasting of Latin American coffees, Colombians are relatively easy to identify. They are much heavier in body than high-grown Central Americans; their flavors are usually murky, and often a bit grassy. Generic Colombians ("UGQ," which stands for usual good quality), be they *supremo* (large beans) or *excelso* (smaller beans), are decent, full-bodied coffees. Many roasters consider these coffees "good blenders" because they're inexpensive and of acceptable quality, but not distinguished in flavor.

When you find a regionally designated Colombian coffee, take it as a good sign. It means you are buying from someone who cares enough to ferret out something exceptional, even from a country whose coffees are going to sell themselves anyway.

If body is what you're looking for, a fine Bucaramanga will offer you the Andean equivalent of Sumatra's fullness. The Nariño region produces balanced coffees with fine acidity and body, and unusually distinctive flavors which may include an agreeable black-walnut bitterness. Coffees from the Huila region feature an intense fruity acidity that complements their full body.

These regionally designated Colombians may be hard to find, but they are the living links to archetypal Colombian flavor. Like the towering mountains in which they grow, they are rugged and large scale, offering heft rather than finesse as their virtue. Although they lack the complexity, clarity, and elegance of the finest Centrals, high-quality Colombians can still provide plenty of luscious enjoyment.

Costa Rica *(Wet-Processed)*

A seasoned coffee pro once said that Costa Rica is to Guatemala what Switzerland is to Italy. Costa Rica processes coffee with the same regimented attention the Swiss give their watches, while processing norms in Guatemala are as relaxed as, say, an Italian after lunch. Costa Rica sets the world standard for consistently high quality in both its wet processing and dry milling. The majority of the processing is done in larger mills using precise quality-control procedures. The best producers recognize a dozen or more distinct qualitative separations during milling, versus two in most Central American nations.

Most Costa Rican coffee comes from the modern hybrid *caturra*, which yields large quantities of good coffee. Some would say that Costa Rican coffee could be even better if more of the older *bourbon* and *typica* types were planted. Perhaps this is true, but given that top Costa Ricans already set the standard by which the rest of Latin America's coffees are measured, such innovations are understandably not a top priority.

The country's best offerings are grown in two especially mountainous areas. The first of these regions is the Tres Rios area near the Pacific coast, which has become well known because of its proximity to railroad lines and the capital, San Jose. Tres Rios coffees are as accessible in flavor as they are geographically; the best coffees are mild, sweet, and flawless with bright acidity and great consistency from cup to cup. Two of the more famous green-coffee marks from this region are Bella Vista and La Magnolia.

The second region is the rugged Tarrazu region, located high in the interior mountains. This area is without question the home of Costa Rica's two greatest coffees.

Tarrazu beans impart heavier body than Tres Rios varieties, along with a sculpted aromatic complexity. Coffee from the La Minita estate is the reference standard for elegant, restrained Tarrazu character, with a purity of flavor few coffees anywhere in the world even approach.

Higher and still more remote is the Dota Tarrazu area. Sold under the trademark Dota Conquistador, its premier offering is a compelling, forceful coffee with notes of chocolate, tropical fruit, and a multidimensional, vinous acidity kissed by the honey (*miel*) of the fermentation tanks.

El Salvador *(Wet-Processed)*

Imagine remote highland valleys replete with greenery and wildlife, acre upon acre of heirloom bourbon and artfully planted shade trees, and precisely delineated farms run by growers dedicated to the highest possible quality. Antigua, Guatemala? Try again: Santa Ana, El Salvador.

The rich heritage of growers here combined with an infusion of post–civil war rebuilding funds from the European Economic Community has made El Salvador the brightest rising star in Latin America. The best coffees are beautifully prepared and perfectly balanced, with pointed acidity, medium body, enticing sweetness, and depth.

This characterization currently applies to the superb estate and cooperative coffees marketed under the Itzalco Premium banner, including those from farms such as Pacas, El Borbollón, and Los Ausoles. These coffees are processed to exacting standards, and stand in sharp contrast to the bulk of Salvadoran production—which consists of neutral, attractively priced blending coffees.

El Salvador is also home to a well-organized cooperative that produces one of the best and most consistent certified organic coffees, under the Pipil brand name. The largest part of the crop goes to Europe. This coffee is 100 percent typica, and its SHG (strictly high grown) grade is excellent.

Guatemala *(Wet-Processed)*

This beautiful country produces more distinctive regional coffees than any other Central American nation. The only region known to most consumers is Antigua; these are often, but by no means always, the best coffees produced in the country. Genuine Antiguas are always costly. Such is the cachet of the name, in fact, that a much greater volume of "Antigua" is sold at retail than is actually produced.

Genuine Antiguas offer a unique blend of high-grown acidity, deep body, and Belgian chocolate flavors edged with smoky spice. At their best, they are perhaps the most complex and compelling coffees of the continent. Quality varies widely from year to year, farm to farm, but some of the established producers whose names you might encounter include San Sebastian, San Miguel, San Rafael Urias, Bella Carmona, and Café Pulcal.

Guatemala's tremendous diversity of microclimates and large number of dedicated growers means there are many riches beyond Antigua worthy of discovery. Coffees from the magical and stunning highlands around Lake Atitlán have a tremendous "top end" of aroma and acidity—so much so that more than one bag has been smuggled across the mountains to enliven off-vintage Antiguas.

The ruggedly mountainous Huehuetenango area ("hue" is pronounced "way") near the Mexican border produces superb coffees as well, full of lively acidity and an orange-peel fruitiness. The remote Cobán region's legendary coffees are very rarely seen in the United States because of the strong demand from long-established European buyers. These coffees are grown in the wettest, mistiest conditions imaginable. Their resultant delicacy and wild fruitiness is so pronounced as to be more reminiscent of Ethiopian coffees than of other Guatemalans. The current reference-standard coffees from this region are called Pocola and Santa Cecilia. The better farmers in these and several other up-and-coming areas have large stands of heirloom bourbon coffee (some are even going so far as to rip out existing plots of higher-yielding hybrids).

Because processing methods are relatively unsophis-ticated even in the best of cases, sourcing top Guatemalans is somewhat maddening for roasters. Nevertheless, the search is eminently worthwhile and, in the best years, uncovers coffees that represent the ideal balance of nature and nurture. We look forward to a time when the specialty market has evolved such that merchants will feature not only Antigua's coffees but a colorful range of other regional Guatemalan offerings as well.

Honduras *(Wet-Processed)*

Like El Salvador and Mexico, Honduras is mostly considered as a source for cheap blending coffees—when it is considered at all. Some in the trade refer to Honduran coffees as "Colombian substitutes" (faint praise indeed). As in so many other places, there are excellent coffees grown here, but getting them out of the country before they are blended with lesser beans is always a problem.

With numerous good farms and knowledgeable farmers, as well as large stands of heirloom arabica trees, Honduras has a good chance of reaching more specialty coffee drinkers as the market matures.

Mexico *(Wet-Processed)*

Mexico produces large quantities of sound but somewhat unremarkable coffee, most of which is a good fit for cost-conscious blending and dark roasting. Good, high-grown, or *altura,* coffees from Mexico are characteristically light-bodied and nutty. The better examples have a milk chocolate-like tang and delicacy—well suited for a light first cup of the day.

Small amounts of world-class coffee with much greater acidity and flavor intensity are produced in the high mountains of Oaxaca, Veracruz, and Chiapas, but, here again, extracting them before they are blended requires monumental effort. Several importers and roasters have risen to the challenge of importing and featuring these special coffees, which are usually designated by farm name once they arrive. Some of the best small farm coffees, incidentally, are also certified as organically grown.

Nicaragua *(Wet-Processed)*

Land of great poets, tragic civil wars, lakes and mountains, hope and tenacity, Nicaragua has the potential to produce coffees that are second to none. The coffee trade there, like the country overall, is currently working to rebuild itself. Coffee farming promises to save displaced farmers from urban squalor and return them to the countryside, while bringing desperately needed cash into the country.

Some decades past, coffees from Nicaragua's premier growing regions of Jinotega and Matagalpa were legendary for their quality. There is no doubt that the country possesses the soil, microclimates, coffee types, and skilled farmers necessary to rise to such heights again. Today's good-quality, high-grown Nicaraguan coffees are typically bold (meaning very large) beans with a pronounced, sometimes almost salty acidity. They have the heavier body for which Caribbean coffees have earned renown and simple, satisfying flavors. This profile is sometimes marred by a bit of past-crop woodiness or other flavor taint caused by the cumbersome traditional processing system.

Historically, coffees have been washed and partially dried on farms before being blended, machine-dried, and processed by exporters, who don't always give individual coffees the attention they need and deserve. Generally, however, prices are still more than fair for the quality, making these coffees a good choice for blending and the application of darker roast styles.

Panama *(Wet-Processed)*

At their best, Panamanian coffees are very similar to Costa Rican coffees from the Tres Rios region. Sweet, bright, balanced, and neutral to a fault, they are useful blenders and, in the case of the top farm- or estate-designated coffees, provide ideal mild breakfast brews.

A handful of top producers have dedicated themselves to producing coffees whose purity and intensity of flavor— and price—matches the top Costa Ricans and Guatemalans. These estate-designated coffees are definitely worth trying.

Peru *(Wet-Processed)*

Not a world-class producer by any standard, Peru is known for its cheap, treacherous (that is, likely to be tainted with ferment or other serious defects) coffees. The best of these are reasonably sound French roast material. Most Peruvian coffee is processed by small producers with little understanding of quality control.

The notable reason Peruvian coffees have become widely available is that Peru is a principle player in the recent surge of "commodity organics." These coffees sell for a specialty coffee price purely on the strength of the causes they support and not on the basis of cup quality. Even the better Peruvian coffees belong in a can, not a specialty store.

GEOGRAPHICALLY MISPLACED AND MEDIOCRE: HAWAIIAN AND CARIBBEAN COFFEES

The interesting coffees from this area are, truthfully and despite their reputations to the contrary, few and far between. None are world class. Some—most notably Jamaican Blue Mountain and coffees from Puerto Rico— have been marketing themselves as producers of high-quality specialty coffee. These coffees are primarily distinguished, however, by their high price and disappointingly mediocre flavor.

In a blind cupping of fine coffees from around the world, the stunningly expensive coffees of Jamaica and Hawaii rank right at the bottom—just about equal in quality to a well-prepared Mexican or Costa Rican blending coffee that typically commands only a tenth, or even a twentieth, of the price.

So how does anyone get away with such inflated prices? Marketing mystique, and the pervasive belief that quality is indicated by rarity and cost. The fact that many people first encounter Hawaiian, Jamaican, and Puerto Rican coffees on their honeymoons and holidays surely enhances the appeal of these coffees as well. One should take into account that these countries incur significantly higher production costs than most, due to higher wage standards and astronomical real estate values. That said, be warned that any savvy coffee buyer would regard the gift of a pound of Jamaican Blue Mountain or Kona as one step away from a coal in his proverbial stocking!

Hawaii *(Wet-Processed)*

Kona is, of course, the most famous name, but these days there are also newly minted offerings from the islands of Maui and Molokai. These latter have reached their goal of providing Kona-like flavor for half the price. Where all of these islands are concerned, however, "there ain't no mountain high enough" to produce coffee worthy of the premiums they are demanding

The biggest, boldest grades of Kona (Fancy and Extra Fancy) are gorgeous to look at, the beans so bold and even that they almost seem artificial. In the cup, however, even the finest small-farm Konas—which are far superior to the bulked offerings of the island's larger exporters—offer simple, mild flavors, slight acidity, and medium body. There are descriptions written that flatter Kona as, "wonderfully aromatic," but its aromas pale in comparison to Kenya, Ethiopian Yergacheffe, Yemen Mocha, and others.

If you do feel compelled to try Kona, go the distance to get fresh, 100 percent unblended coffee. (If you really want to taste it, you will have to.) Blends including Kona abound, most craftily labeled so as to appear pure. But given its delicate nature, few coffees in the world are more ill-suited to this practice; once blended, a true Kona disappears,

Jamaican Blue Mountain *(Wet-Processed)*

Twenty years ago, choice lots of Jamaican Blue Mountain were superb. Offering pungently nutty aroma, fine acidity, and a unique beef bouillon-like flavor, this coffee staked out a truly persistent reputation. Today, the results of over-production and a marked lack of attention to cup quality throughout the stages of processing and export handling make even authentic Blue Mountain coffees mediocre at best. The lesser Jamaican grades, "high mountain" and "prime," are still expensive and surpassed in flavor by virtually every other specialty coffee.

For a taste of the contemporary coffee that's closest to what Jamaican once was, try Papua New Guinea—much of which has been cultivated using Blue Mountain seed stock.

Dominican Republic, Haiti, Puerto Rico, and Cuba (Wet-Processed)

Growing at moderate altitudes, the coffees from these countries are rich and full-bodied with decent acidity and uncomplicated flavors. They are ideally suited for the moderately dark-roasted espresso blends in which they have traditionally been used.

Dominican and Cuban coffees are priced realistically enough that such blending is still possible. Unfortunately, the Puerto Rican and Haitian coffees offered within the specialty market in the United States are expensive and not worth the price. Puerto Rican coffee is heavily marketed with the romantic beaches of the island at the core of its message; Haitian beans are offered for sale on a platform of social causes.

We mean to question neither the appeal nor the tragic history of these countries, but to maintain that there are more appropriate indicators of coffee quality. Based solely on performance in the cup, these coffees do not merit being offered to consumers in unblended form.

AFRICA AND ARABIA

While Latin American coffees are accessible, Africans and Arabians are original. Set out cups of Kenya, Yemen Mocha, Ethiopian Harrar, and Yergacheffe for a blind tasting, and even a neophyte coffee taster can distinguish and name them. Try a similar exercise with a range of Central American coffees, and you will see seasoned professionals fail to do the same.

Coffee still grows wild in Ethiopia, its native land, and tribesmen harvest the berries. Across the Red Sea lies Yemen, which in ancient times was called Arabic (whence *arabica*). This is the land where coffee first made the transition from wild bush to cultivated crop, and the coffee there today is grown by the descendants of those who discovered the magical transformation achieved by cooking the seeds of the coffee cherry. These natural, organically grown coffees have a complexity and rusticity no others in the world can match.

At the other end of the spectrum lie Kenya and its East African neighbors, producers of ultra-modern washed coffees. Despite their consistency, these offerings are still replete with the exotic, vivid, and uniquely African aromas and flavors.

Ethiopia *(Dry- or Wet-Processed)*
A wide range of dry- and wet-processed coffees are produced in Ethiopia. The quality of these varies widely. This makes cupping expertise all the more critical to ferreting out the green coffee gems, but the search is worth it; the best Ethiopian coffees are unsurpassed in their intensity and distinctive flavors.

The best and most costly of the dry-processed coffees comes from the highlands surrounding the medieval city of Harrar. Classic Harrars offer a veritable cornucopia of aromas—cinnamon, wood, spice, and above all blueberry—which can fill a room with perfume. The coffee's flavors match its aroma: winy and berry-like, with good body and plenty of acidity. Unfortunately, the classic samples are few and far between; one more typically encounters Harrars that feature the characteristics of less expensive Ethiopians such as Jimmas or Lekempti.

Both of these coffees are dominated by burlap-like flavors. "Rustic" is too polite a word for them, but the traditional descriptor, "gamy," comes close. Lekempti often displays the two most watched-for coffee defects, ferment and hardness, simultaneously! If you like to walk on the wild side, you will enjoy exploring these coffees, but most coffee drinkers would do well to heed the message in Harrar's traditional trade designation: "the poor man's (Yemen) Mocha."

Fine washed-process Ethiopian coffees are every bit as inconsistent as the naturals, but the best examples are stunning. Yergacheffe *can* be one of the most outstanding; in theory, Yergacheffe is an especially fine part of the overall production of the idyllic Sidamo region, where coffee is grown organically in pristine forest conditions. Given the Byzantine realities of commerce in today's Ethiopia, however, coffees sold under the less specific name of Sidamo may be as good as or better than a Yergacheffe. Rather than concentrating on names, we urge you to embrace this mission: Find the coffee that, when roasted and freshly ground, imparts a fragrance so penetrating that brewing hardly seems necessary!

More than any other coffee, Yergacheffe is about aroma. Properly roasted (and for this coffee, that means relatively lightly), a superlative sample offers a seductive, almost perfumed aroma of lemon peel laced with honeysuckle and apricot. The flavor is almost mentholated, while the body is light and elegant.

Because of problems with the washing process and the mixing of different lots, Yergacheffes and Sidamos often fall short of their potential for intensity. One also sees quite a few samples with defective beans blended in. If you find yourself disappointed initially, keep trying; great Yergacheffe is among the top half-dozen coffees in the world. Be on the lookout for exceptional coffees from the neighboring Limu region as well, which can offer similar acidity and flavors.

Yemen Mocha *(Dry-Processed)*

This is archetypal coffee, for within a single cup of Mocha one may glimpse all the flavors coffee grown the world over has to offer. You may find bright acidity; musky, wine-in-a-barrel fruitiness; earth and sweet spice; roasted nuts; chocolate; wood; or tobacco. The variations in flavor can be maddening, or intriguing. Every cup, every pot, every purchased lot is different.

What you get is the sum total of ripeness at the time of harvesting, which in Yemen happens when the majority—but not all—of the beans have reached their peak. The coffee is stripped from the trees and dried on mats or bare ground in the long Arabian sun. Sufficiently dry, the cherries are winnowed by crude mortar and delivered to roasters in a refreshing state of naturalness.

The best contemporary Mochas come from a small area in Bany Matar province (called Mattari) or from the steep,

arid hillsides around the capital of San'a (Sanani). Sanani
Mochas generally boast a more "top end" wildness and
fruity character, while Mattaris yield extra body and
chocolate. With these coffees, the skill of individual roasters
is particularly critical to coaxing the full range of nuances
from the beans. Price is one guide to authenticity, but
though expensive, a strong argument can be made that these
are among the best values in coffee on a strictly pleasure-
per-pound basis.

Kenya *(Wet-Processed)*

A relentless focus on quality makes Kenya the pacesetter for
washed coffees. A "regular" Kenya AA (AA being the
designation for the largest, most evenly graded bean) is
almost invariably an excellent cup of coffee, clean and full
bodied with impressive acidity. This sort of Kenya is used to
improve the quality of more neutral Latin American coffees
in high-profile European blends, and it is also the easiest
type of Kenya to find in U.S. specialty stores. But it's just
the beginning.

The Great Kenyan coffees are grown on small farms which
wet-process their coffee cooperatively. The small, individual
lots from these co-ops typically amount to only 20 to 70
bags of coffee during the main crop season. (These co-ops
are the true producers of coffees labeled "Estate Kenya.")

The coffees are purchased by bidding on individual lots
at the Kenyan auctions in Nairobi, which are held every
Tuesday during their season. Competition for the top lots is
fierce, and the very best of these coffees can easily cost twice
as much as the very good quality "normal" AA's. There is no
coffee on earth more deserving of the premiums, however;
the superlative offerings yield plush, almost decadent body,

astonishing red-wine acidity, and heaps of black-currant flavor and aroma. Drink one of these coffees, and you may find yourself agreeing with many professional tasters—a top Kenya makes most other coffees taste ordinary.

The Kenyan coffee production system is unique, with a structure that rewards farmers directly for achieving top quality. Coffees to be offered for sale are first sent to the chief taster at the Kenya Coffee Board, who cups them blind and assigns a rating based on standardized criteria for bean preparation, flavor, acidity, and aroma. Samples are then air-expressed to potential buyers, and these buyers or their agents are able to bid on specific lots. Quality remains high, because expectations on both the buying and selling sides are rigorous and mutually consistent.

While Kenya is without a doubt Africa's quality leader and a standard-setter for the rest of the world, there have been worrisome indications of decline in recent years. When world market prices are low, quality suffers; the use of fertilizers, proper pruning techniques, and other growing aids declines.

The negative effects have been exacerbated by the introduction of a higher-yielding, disease-resistant hybrid called Ruiru 11, which is intended to supplement the traditional Kenyan arabica varieties. The current percentage of these plants in use is small, but pure samples of it cupped in recent years taste like low-grade coffee from a completely different country.

Several American coffee experts, most notably George Howell, founder of Boston's Coffee Connection and perhaps the country's leading advocate for coffee quality, are working with Kenyan authorities to ensure that traditional varieties continue to be cultivated. The key, as always, is for coffee lovers who care about quality to "ante up" with the higher prices required for growing the best.

Zimbabwe, Burundi, and Malawi *(Wet-Processed)*

From a taster's point of view, all of these coffees live under the giant shadow cast by Kenya. They come across as junior versions of their intensely acidic, big-bodied neighbor— which makes them appealing choices for those who like East African fruit and acidity in less Herculean doses. Very few of these coffees are complete or balanced enough to merit straight consumption, especially when great Kenyas and washed Ethiopians are available.

That said, there are some budding estates to watch for. Two farms in particular deserve special mention: the Smaldeel Estate in Zimbabwe and Mapanga in Malawi, both of which produce impeccably prepared coffees with excellent acidity, body, and balance. These coffees have improved every year and are worthy of consideration by consumers looking for a mild but still very flavorful sip of washed East African coffee.

INDONESIA

Only about a dozen of Indonesia's 13,677 islands produce coffee, which was first introduced by Dutch traders to this area in 1696. Java, of course, is the most well-known— primarily because the Dutch cultivated trees there first. As recently as 50 years ago, all Indonesian coffee was sold as Java, despite the fact that only a relatively small portion of it actually came from the island.

Today, Indonesia is the world's third-largest producer of coffee, but over 90 percent of the total crop from Indonesia is robusta. The great arabicas of Sumatra, Sulawesi (formerly called Celebes), and Java, which specialty coffee drinkers think of as prototypically Indonesian, are actually quite rare and obscure from a commercial standpoint.

The Indonesians draw devotees with an herby, earthy range of flavors. Gone are the acidity and high notes of the Central Americas, the wine and fruit of Africa. Instead, these are contemplative coffees. They offer tantalizing, entrancing hints of crushed autumn leaves, wood smoke, and wild mushrooms.

Estate Java *(Wet-Processed)*

After many years of declining quality, Javanese coffees are undergoing a revival. Java is a coffee that offers a pure experience of body; it can seem almost oily or syrupy when the roast is dark enough. The flavors are relatively simple, with a pleasing nuttiness and subtle hints of black pepper and leather.

As washed coffees, contemporary Javas do not have the more classic Indonesian forest-floor flavors found in Sumatra and Sulawesi. It is exactly this absence, however, that makes Javas all the more useful in blends, where they are able to contribute weight without funk.

Sumatra and Sulawesi *(Dry-Processed)*

The really great coffees come from Sumatra and Sulawesi. They are massive and full-bodied—low in acidity and heavy in body. Produced on small family farms averaging less than three acres in size, coffee grows alongside fruit, spices, and other food crops. It is not unusual to see dried cherries spread along the road for winnowing under the tires of passing vehicles.

This tradition results in tremendous variation in quality from region to region and year to year. For this reason, the critical eye and discerning palate of the green-coffee importer and buyer are that much more important in ensuring the quality of what reaches the consumer.

Technically, some coffees from these islands are "semi-washed." This means that water is used during initial processing, but the final product exhibits more classic, dry-processed coffee flavors because of the intermixing of coffee types and relatively indiscriminate dry milling.

Sumatras are smooth. High-quality Sumatras are enormously full-bodied with a pronounced herbal aroma and a dry, almost alkaline quality to them. By experimenting with Sumatras from different roasters—that is to say, by trying Sumatras at different degrees of roast—you can dial in to your own preference for the expression of this coffee's earthiness and funk. Some select Sumatras are so clean and elegant that they taste almost like washed coffees. Others are so outrageously earthy that if they are not roasted to a surface color dangerously close to charcoal, they simply cannot be consumed.

At their finest, Sulawesis are considered the best of the very best of the Indonesians. Rather than the dry quality of Sumatras, they possess a seductive combination of butter-caramel sweetness and herbaceous, loamy tastes. These two qualities, though distinct, are inseparable. Coffees from Sulawesi are earthy, complex, and generous, with deep body that resembles maple syrup more closely than anything else. They are more expensive than Sumatran varieties because of their small yields and the consistently fierce buying competition from Japan.

Aged Coffees: Sumatra, Java, and Sulawesi
There's another theme that surfaces when you keep your eyes open to Indonesians in the marketplace. On rare and celebrated occasions, beans from these three islands are offered as aged coffees.

Once the Dutch had Indonesian coffee production in full swing, the inevitable occurred. Surplus beans started piling up. Held in the thick, wet heat of government plantations, the extras began changing color. They turned yellow after two to three years, and then progressed to a deep shade of brown.

In most producing countries, coffee in such condition would simply be considered frightfully "past crop," defeatingly bland without its acidity and destined to act as a low-profile filler for institutional blends. Not so these coffees. The aging process emphasizes the earthy, spicy notes of the Indonesians so dramatically that even unroasted samples carry the uniquely heady aromas of cedar, tobacco, and oriental spices. The reduction in acidity results in a mellowing that many find profoundly pleasing.

Papua New Guinea *(Wet-Processed)*
Here you have a coffee with a history as fascinating as its taste. The original 1927 plantings used Jamaican Blue Mountain seedlings, which were nestled in the island's spectacular high-elevation swamps. At about 5,000 to 6,000 feet, these seedlings flourished in incredibly good soil and produced coffee with more complexity and flavor than the best Jamaican Blue ever had.

This coffee is fabulous and fascinating at multiple degrees of roast. What you get with the best Papua New Guineas is a pungent, mango and papaya fruitiness in the aroma. A large-scale, perfectly balanced coffee with superb acidity, pungent nutty aroma, clean flavor, and extremely full body, Papua New Guinea perfectly synthesizes the fruit and zing of Latin American with the depth and warmth of Indonesia. It is probably the most versatile blending coffee in the world (when cost is no object, that is).

The best of these coffees are plantation-grown, the most famous of which include Sigri and Arona. New Guinea is also the source of a world class, certified organically grown coffee sold under the Okapa brand name.

THE HONORARY INDONESIAN

India *(Wet-Processed)*

This legendary producer of fine teas is also an important coffee producer, and was in fact the first country outside Africa and Arabia to begin cultivating coffee. Most of the production is lower-quality institutional-grade coffee, but transitions in the Indian coffee market over recent years have made a tiny trickle of world-class coffees available. If you love Indonesians, you will find Indian coffees to be worth a special search. They offer similar body and different but highly complementary flavors.

Fine Indian coffees are produced in the states of Karnatka (formerly Mysore), Kerala, and Tamilnadu (formerly Madras). The best plantation-grown coffees from these areas are washed arabicas, which in good crop years offer Guatemalan-like acidity and cocoa notes. These characteristics are anchored by a body fullness reminiscent of Javan coffee, and illuminated by the uniquely Indian spice flavors of nutmeg, clove, cardamom, and pepper.

In many areas, these and other spices grow right beside the coffee, resulting in what one might call a flavored coffee for purists! These coffees are intriguing on their own, and can also be used to add valuable lushness and spice to premium espresso blends.

Fans of aged Indonesians like Sumatra and Sulawesi will also want to experience India's famous "monsooned" coffees, which have been exposed, under carefully controlled conditions, to the sea air and high humidity of the monsoon season itself. Appealing to those who shun acidity in favor of the earthier range of flavors, monsooned coffees have a distinct woody, briny quality.

Roasting and Blending

Master roasters view the work of roasting and blending as facilitation, not creation. No one who has visited a coffee farm dedicated to producing top-quality coffee can doubt that the majority of the work required to make great coffee occurs there. Great coffees bear the invisible imprint of the hundreds of pairs of hands that have touched them on their journey from seedling to roast-ready green bean. And, like making wine from the grapes of a centuries-old grand cru vineyard, possession of such rarefied raw material obliges one to do it justice.

Roasting "to Taste" and Tasting to Roast

To roast coffee artfully, you must taste ("cup") it constantly, and vice versa. Roasting and tasting go together like breathing and living; they're that close. It is easy enough to roast coffee by the numbers, using a thermometer and basic guidelines. But true artisan roasting is achieved only when each coffee at one's disposal has been tasted thoughtfully, and at a wide range of roasts, prior to final selection of the optimum production roast for that coffee. (A "production" roast is the roast used on coffee intended for the larger marketplace. "Sample" roasts are used to examine the specific characteristics of a green coffee being considered by a roaster for purchase, and vary based on the specific characteristics under scrutiny.)

The tasting process continues with the regular cupping of production roasts. Because green coffee changes character with the passage of time—it fades during the months it is held in inventory, then suddenly rejuvenates, vibrant with acidity, when new crop time arrives—good coffee roasters must taste their production constantly to ensure the consistency of the final product.

THE RELATIVITY OF ROAST STYLE

The degree of roast applied should always be relative to the potential of the coffee being roasted, and invariably ends up being relative to the roaster who controls the process as well. As one accomplished green-coffee roaster describes, "In finding the perfect path for the coffee to express itself, one finds oneself."

Green coffee beans are literally seeds of potential flavor, each with its own particular nature. A fine dry-processed Brazilian bean, for example, is physically soft and fragile. It needs a delicate application of heat to bring out its best. This type of bean realizes its full flavor potential early in the roasting process and turns charred and burnt at temperatures that are just commencing to bring out the best in some harder, higher-grown, washed coffees. Representatives of the latter type, coffees such as Guatemalan Antigua and Papua New Guinea, are highly prized by roasters for their chameleon-like ability to display enjoyable yet distinctly different flavors at a wider variety of roasts.

At the very light and dark ends of the roasting spectrum, coffee flavors are simple. At one extreme, the infamous American canned-coffee "cinnamon" roast touts a grassy, green, and cereal-like flavor. On the other end, the darkest "French" roast imparts pure char, with a hint of oily fishiness. Between these two, there is an enormously wide range of roast styles available.

As you already know, roast name is not an objective indicator of roast degree. When we use roast names in this book, we are incorporating both the traditional trade definitions and our own knowledge of roasting as reference points. Your job as a coffee lover is to rise above all the jargon and find roasters who handle their coffees skillfully, roasting them in a way—no matter what they call it—that emphasizes the characteristics most pleasing to you. The following description of the roasting process may help you get your bearings.

WHAT HAPPENS DURING ROASTING?

From start to finish, a roast typically takes 10 to 15 minutes. Over the course of the process, the green coffee being roasted loses between 12 percent and 25 percent of the weight it possessed going in, depending on the specific type of coffee and the degree of the roast applied.

The roasting machines used by most specialty roasters look like oversized clothes dryers. These are often called "batch" roasters, and they have capacities ranging from a dozen to several hundred pounds. The green beans are poured into a large, barrel-like chamber that has been carefully preheated (most roasters are gas-fired).

The beans are spun in the cylinder to heat them evenly, while the roaster monitors their progress by time, temperature (thermometers measure both bean and air temperature), sight, smell, and sound. The all-important visual and auditory feedback is achieved by means of a small, trough-like probe called a "tryer." The tryer permits roasters to pull samples of beans from the drum at any point during roasting.

When the roaster judges a roast to have reached its peak, she opens the door on the front of the machine and allows the beans to cascade into a cooling tray. A broad paddle arm sweeps through the beans, spreading them over a perforated screen while a powerful fan draws air through the lot.

One of the basic exercises roaster trainees go through at Allegro Coffee Company in Boulder, Colorado, is called "tasting progressive roasts." They take a top-quality coffee and sample roast it a dozen ways, then cup each sample. Repeating the process with every coffee in the warehouse begins to shape the tools necessary for conscious roasting.

Let's take one of these coffees—a Guatemalan Antigua, perhaps—and follow it through from raw green bean to French roast.

Zero to Six Minutes

After the bean enters the roaster, it appears as though nothing happens for the first few minutes. Crucial changes

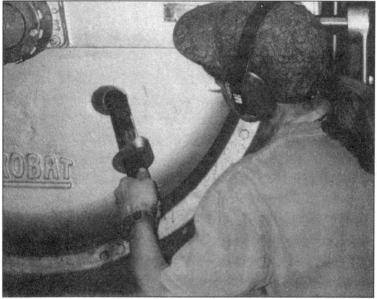

Photos ©1995 by Kevin Knox

Top: Green beans in the warehouse await roasting. Bottom: The tryer permits roasters to pull samples from the drum during roasting.

are occurring, however. Water boils and is driven off at 212°F; pyrolysis of sugars (chemical decomposition as a result of heat) begins at 266°F.

Right around the 3-minute mark, the green coffee brightens from the application of heat. A couple of minutes later, the beans turn yellow. At this point, nothing looks much like the coffee we know; the smells are of grass, hay, and cereal.

Seven to Eight Minutes: "First Pop"

At about 7 minutes the beans, which have by now turned light tan, pop open like popcorn and swell to twice their previous size. The remaining sliver of protective silverskin on each bean, called "chaff," flies off and is collected outside the roasting chamber. At this point, the heat applied to the coffee is lowered.

If the roast is terminated here, which it is by many canned coffee purveyors for reasons of cost, we will be left with what is called a "cinnamon roast." For Guatemalan Antigua, that means a cup with almost undrinkable lemon-like acidity and not a whole lot else. So we persevere—and from here, the coffee changes quickly and demands the full attention of the person roasting it.

Nine to Eleven Minutes: Ripening to Full City

Over the next minute or two, the coffee rapidly changes color and the popping gradually subsides. After cinnamon we reach the even, light brown "city roast" stage, which then ripens into the chestnut of classic "full city."

The classic full city roast has been aptly renamed "full flavor" by master roaster George Howell of Boston because, at this stage, the coffee has developed the most possible body while still retaining peak acidity, aroma, and varietal dimensionality. For those who prize these characteristics in their coffees, it is time to stop.

Now we look and listen to the coffee very carefully, paying particular attention to any hints of the hissing, brittle, percussive sound that indicates the beginning of "second pop." This is a sign that the coffee is turning a corner, heading full speed toward "Vienna roast."

Twelve to Thirteen Minutes: "Second Pop"
Beyond the full city stage, things get exciting. We head full tilt into a much more rapid popping process as the beans' cell walls break down. Natural oils previously suspended in the structure begin to migrate toward the bean surface. We have now entered the realm of Vienna roast, the "sweet spot" wherein acidity is being traded for body; high notes and aromatics, for sweet carmelized sugar tastes.

Flavor gets simpler while body becomes increasingly plush. This Guatemalan Antigua is a grand cru, and it shows its mettle by the way the beans resist the intensity of heat. They slowly turn a bittersweet chocolate brown. We can go a long way into this range before any burnt tastes creep in.

Stop the roast here and you have a cup with heavy, chocolate-like body and spice, with slight but still vital acidity supporting the lushness. We have gone from still wine to port or sherry. As with the full city range, roasters who know this territory well recognize numerous and distinct microtones of color, each corresponding to equally exact flavors.

Master cupper and blender Jim Reynolds of Peet's Coffee and Tea in San Francisco has been perfecting coffees in this realm for a lifetime. His approach has been imitated by many, but largely without success; most others fail to understand the enormous commitment to green-coffee quality this "dancing on the edge" roast style requires.

Fourteen Minutes and Beyond

Second pop is over, and the beans are eerily quiet. Very, very dark brown and glistening with oil, the coffee has uttered its last gasp of varietal uniqueness. This degree of roast is known as "Italian" on the U.S. West Coast (though no one in Italy roasts so dark).

A pronounced smokiness creeps in; bean sugars are carbonizing instead of carmelizing. Another minute or so and the beans are jet black. Watch for blue smoke and keep one eye on the thermometer, or be prepared to call the fire department. We have reached French roast; the beans are 20 percent carbon. The taste of the coffee itself is extinct, the beans serving merely as a vehicle for the power of the roast.

CAN YOU JUDGE A BEAN BY ITS COLOR?

The concise answer is no. You cannot accurately gauge the roast of a bean by its color, nor the quality of a coffee by its degree of roast.

Judging roast by color is just plain dangerous. Without knowing what the constituent coffees were, you can't accurately predict flavors from the color of the result. Decaffeinated coffees provide a good example. As a result of the decaffeination process, they start out military drab. During roasting, they take on various shades of gray and black—yet the actual roast degree may be the same as that applied to caffeinated coffees that still appear much lighter.

The final roast color of Indonesian coffees can prove equally misleading. Because they don't have the same inherent pigmentation Central American coffees have, these coffees look dark and oily even when roasted to the same objective degree as a lighter-looking Central American.

In any case, darker doesn't necessarily mean better. It is true that to succeed in expressing varietal flavors through a longer roast, a roaster must begin by investing in high-quality coffees. But the choicest beans are never consigned to the darkest roasts, even among those most fanatical about quality. Sound but basic coffees are typically used for dark roasts and flavorings—through the cloaks of which less actual coffee taste is discernible, anyway.

There is a certain "rite of passage" quality to drinking ultra-dark-roasted coffees, an initial appeal that smacks of sophistication. Perhaps, as is the case with anything new, we tend to evaluate coffees on the basis of those aspects of quality we can most easily recognize and enumerate. Dramatic but simple, the darker roasts are impressive in a particular and obvious way. They are as forceful and memorable as one's first experience with a habañero pepper. Because of the strength of these associations, many coffee drinkers mistakenly associate good coffee exclusively with the darker styles.

It is interesting to note that the flavors professional cuppers and tasters most dote upon are the bright, fruity, and winey flavors captured only when coffees (such as Kenya, Yergacheffe, and Costa Rica Dota Conquistador) are roasted no darker than full city.

THE "RIGHT" ROAST STYLE

You know by now that roasting is an interpretation of agricultural ingredients; there is no more an "ideal" roast than there is an "ideal" national cuisine. But while most people tend to be somewhat adventurous when it comes to culinary tastes, their approach to coffee is another matter. Consumers quickly become conditioned to prefer a particular roast style, and it is often that of the first well-prepared beverage they taste.

Coffee marketers are well aware of this conditioning process and use it to their advantage. The recent boom of Seattle-style dark roasts is a clear example. Consumers can't help but appreciate the difference between the darker specialty coffees and sour, light-roasted canned types. This leap in quality is startling and gratifying—and causes most coffee drinkers to instantaneously associate their newfound pleasure with the darker degree of roast.

Having formed an attachment to darker-roasted coffees, they are then hesitant to try specialty coffees at lighter roasts. The negative associations with canned coffee lead them to assume that anything but the Seattle-style roasts are inferior in taste and quality.

Our point is that beyond these darker introductory experiences lies a world of coffee flavors—those optimized rather than disguised by roast. Fruit and flowers, spice and sweetness... Coffee has much more to show us than simply strong or weak, dark or light.

Tasting note: Here is a not-to-be missed tasting trinity that shows the multiple ways in which coffee can be "strong": French roast, Sumatra, and Kenya. The French roast is smoky and aggressive, but light-bodied; the Sumatra offers heft and body without bitterness; and Kenya's power comes from its pronounced acidity and fruit.

MATCHING ROAST STYLE WITH BREWING PREFERENCE

We have discussed the importance of matching roast degree to an individual coffee's flavor potential. A more subtle point that escapes the conscious attention of even seasoned coffee lovers is the reward of matching roast to one's chosen brewing method.

There are many ways to brew coffee. You may already know which offerings taste best when brewed at home with your plunger pot or drip coffee maker. You may know which coffee of the day you're happiest to see on the menu board of your local café. You may also attribute this to the coffee alone, without taking the brewer into account. *But the brewing method you use has everything to do with determining what coffees you enjoy most while using it.*

For example, the vacuum pot is a uniquely pure vehicle for appreciating the high notes, aroma, and varietal nuance of a coffee. Drip-brewed coffee highlights these same qualities, although use of a paper filter mutes the aromatics slightly. Ideal choices for these brewers are coffees with lots of aroma: a fine Central American, a Kenyan or an Ethiopian Yergacheffe, roasted no darker than traditional full city.

A coffee press yields a coffee that is above all heavy-bodied; at the same time, the slight but definite pressure exerted as the metal filter is plunged through the slurry of grounds and water increases the perceived acidity of the coffee. This method shines when matched with coffees whose strong suit is lush body imparted by both bean and roast; lighter roasts of higher-acid coffees can be overwhelming. A dependable classic to try is a Vienna-roasted Indonesian coffee such as Sumatra.

Finally, there is espresso. Because of the tremendously high pressure used during brewing and the scant amount of concentrated liquid that results, this method requires the most specialized bean and roast combinations of them all. The acidity of the coffee must be reduced to virtually nothing, since the pressurized extraction highlights perceived acidity enormously. On the other hand, this method also accentuates roasty bitterness dramatically. The right coffee for espresso is neither very lightly nor extremely darkly roasted, and has been formulated, tasted, tested, and retested specifically on and for an espresso machine.

Artisan Blending

A blend, simply said, is a combination of coffees from different countries. Blend names, while sometimes fanciful, often provide an indication of the character of the blend or the circumstances under which it is designed to be enjoyed.

A great blend has an ideal, a specific and complex flavor profile associated with it. In this way, a blend is like the dish an illustrious and inventive chef might concoct. One starts with the vision in mind and works backward to create it. The specific ingredients—the coffee beans—used to formulate that vision will be reapportioned, roasted differently, or substituted as their own flavor characteristics vary.

At its best, an artfully composed blend offers complexity and consistency of flavor that few straight coffees can match. Such artisan blending is the expression of a master taster's understanding of the flavor potential of all the unblended coffees the world produces—at many different degrees of roast. It is an old cliché but a true one: A great blend is one that yields more than the sum of its parts.

BLENDING BASICS

In its ideal form, the world's first and most famous coffee blend, Mocha Java, illustrates one of the most important principles of blending: blending based on *complementary* ingredients, with an end result that is smooth and unified. Yemen Mocha is a coffee with lots of flavor and aroma, but only medium body. Java's strong suit is its body, but its flavors are relatively simple. Combine the two in the right percentages and you have characteristics neither alone will ever provide. Mocha Java is a coffee that is balanced and pleasing in all respects: flavor, acidity, and body.

Blending based on *contrast* plays up the differences between coffees. Classic examples of this principle are the Scandinavian and Viennese blends, which use a percentage of dark roast to spice up a lightly roasted base of bright Latin American coffees. The opposing tastes, typified by the acidity of the base and the smokiness of the dark roast, are intriguing and palate cleansing once combined.

By now, you probably have the picture: Great blends are inspired by the inherently nuanced and dramatic flavors of varietal coffees. And to be a proficient blender, you have to know your ingredients. Having tasted every coffee in the warehouse numerous times at a wide range of roasts, you must then hold this information in your head—and on your palate—in order to create the combinations that work.

Blending is laborious, and the handful of roasters that do it well fashion dozens, even hundreds, of permutations before settling on and sending a blend to the marketplace.

PRE- AND POST-ROAST BLENDING

Green coffees may be blended together before roasting, as in the case of pre-roast blending, or afterwards, which is called post-roast blending. Master roasters use both pre- and post-roast blending to come up with just the right combination. The question of pre- versus post-roast blending is not an issue of which method is better, but rather which is more appropriate in a given situation.

Blending prior to roasting makes sense—and works well—only when the coffees to be blended are compatible in density and behavior during roasting. For example, you might combine high-grown Guatemalan and Costa Rican beans and roast them to a uniform degree. Mixing either of these coffees with a soft, dry-processed Brazil or Sumatra before roasting, however, would result in a finished batch in which one coffee was over-roasted while the other remained sadly underdeveloped.

Post-roast blending is more labor-intensive and time-consuming than pre-roast blending, and is therefore more expensive. It is also essential to good blending in many instances. The most obvious of these is the making of a blend that includes both dark and light roasts, which by definition must be roasted separately. Less obvious, but no less important, are combinations of coffees whose behavior in the roaster is radically different. Post-roast blending is absolutely necessary for mixing delicate, tricky-to-roast dry-processed coffees such as Yemen Mocha or Sumatra with the hardier, more predictable Latin Americans.

At the most sophisticated level, blending resembles the process of musical composition. It combines soloists (individual coffees) and sections (compatible coffees, roasted together) in service of the composer's (master blender's) vision of the final orchestrated piece.

Many coffee lovers are tempted to try their hand at creating custom blends, and we are almost equally tempted to beg them not to. Our urge is born of experience. Home blenders are often disappointed; in the spirit of adventure, they inevitably combine coffees that were never meant to be joined and therefore yield a flavor profile that is terribly askew. Worse, the coffees chosen for blending may actually dull or mute each other's flavors.

Still and all, it goes against our grain to discourage anyone from experimentation in any form. If you must blend, get to know the component coffees first, and good luck. We suggest you do your initial blending as the professionals do—in conservative amounts!

> *Tasting note:* To develop an understanding of blends and blending, it is a great idea to stage tastings that include a blend and several of its component varietals. You will experience breakthrough recognition of the ways in which blending minimizes some characteristics and highlights others—and how a unique overall balance can be created. Pick a blend off the menu board, and ask someone behind the counter what is in it. Buy several of these and an amount of the blend itself, and slurp away.

It is again worthy of mention that, while there are some great blends to be had, the daily consumption of most coffee connoisseurs consists primarily of the best grand cru unblended coffees—roasted no darker than full city. One might thus say that the experience of these single-origin coffees, which inspire great blends yet ultimately surpass them, is both the beginning and the end of the process of becoming knowledgeable about coffee.

BLENDING AND COMMERCE

Having described blending as the art it should be and occasionally is, we feel obliged to point out some of the less noble purposes of blending.

Blends provide valuable opportunity for cost control. The "art" of blending for most mass-market firms consists of disguising the largest possible amount of poor coffee with the smallest possible amount of good stuff. A substantial amount of money (money that could be invested in buying higher-quality green coffee!) is spent on slick marketing for a particular blend and brand. This has the ultimate fiscal advantage to the roaster of market exclusivity: There is only one place for customers to spend their coffee dollars if they want to drink it again.

Quite frankly, this approach to blending is the predominant one in the commercial and "gourmet" coffee business. You can see it in names such as "Kona Blend," "Jamaican-Style," or supermarket-quality "Mocha Java." These coffees rely on famous names to make them attractive to the consumer and usually contain few if any of the rare and costly beans being romanced.

In addition, roasters who roast every coffee in their lineup to an extreme degree tend to be especially ardent advocates of blends. Why? The varietal nuances, and therefore flavor complexity, of their single-origin coffees has been significantly diminished by the very dark roast style. Blends give consumers the illusion of additional variety.

How to Brew Great Coffee at Home

Brewing coffee is a type of cooking. The finished cup reflects the quality and freshness of its ingredients, coffee and water, as well as the degree of precision with which they were measured and combined. These, in turn, reflect the level of attention and knowledge the cook brings to bear.

Most Americans give far less attention to brewing coffee than they do to cooking any other dish, and as a result they get far less enjoyment from their daily cup. We have spent many years behind the counters of stores that sell beans and carefully brewed coffee, and have heard no comment more frequently than, "I just can't brew coffee this good at home." Anyone armed with a bit of good information and about $50 worth of brewing equipment, however, can make a better cup of coffee at home than can be found at just about any coffee bar.

The goal of brewing coffee is to extract the fullest possible range of desirable flavors and leave the rest behind. Essential to great coffee are these elements: *coffee freshness, grind, water, proportion,* and *holding time.* We will take a close look at each of these variables before moving on to discuss specific brewing methods.

Freshly Roasted Beans

Great coffee starts with freshly roasted beans. Depending on where you live, obtaining fresh coffee may be as simple as walking down the street or challenging enough to prompt ordering by mail.

Over 90 percent of the coffee in this country is sold stale. The simple presence of whole beans is not enough to guarantee superior freshness; such coffee exposed to air (in a bin, for example) is at its best during the first week after roasting. By the end of the second week, it has begun to stale slightly. The coffee still offers decent flavor, but acidity and aroma are becoming muted. It takes several more weeks for serious staling to take hold. And after a month or six weeks, no matter how noble the beans or artful the roast, coffee is reduced permanently to the lowercase "c" variety.

So here's the issue: Freshly roasted coffee produces at least three times its volume in carbon dioxide gas (CO_2). This gas helps to allow fresh coffee what little shelf life it can enjoy, but is also the reason fresh coffee can't be sealed in a can, brick pack, or other totally airtight container. The pressure created will simply explode it. Coffee sold in such containers is typically ground and allowed to "degas," becoming partially stale, for 24 hours prior to packaging.

THE REVOLUTIONARY ONE-WAY VALVE

In the late 1960s, the Italian engineer Luigi Goglio introduced a compromise. He revolutionized coffee packaging by
inventing a one-way valve that could be laminated into
layered, oxygen-impermeable packaging material. (The
packaging material was made of plastic and foil.)

Goglio's valve allows the coffee's CO_2 to escape without
letting oxygen back in, resulting in a method of packaging
that vastly increases the shelf life of high-quality coffee.
Conscientious roasters place freshly roasted beans in these
bags and remove nearly all the remaining oxygen by either
inserting the package in a vacuum chamber or displacing
the oxygen with inert nitrogen gas. The bag is then heat-
sealed and, if the roaster is appropriately fanatical about
freshness, dated.

Thus packaged, the beans will remain largely
indistinguishable from fresh-out-of-the-roaster coffee for at
least three months. It isn't forever, but given that coffee
packaged using any other method—or not at all—gets more
stale by the second, valve-bagged coffees are often the
freshest you can find.

Demand freshness. It is one of the most critical elements
that distinguishes specialty coffee from the ordinary joe.
Don't ever be afraid to ask when coffee was roasted or, if a
retailer received her supply in one-way valve bags
(sometimes called "flavorlock" bags), when the current bag
was opened.

If no one can answer your questions, you are probably
better off buying elsewhere. In some parts of the country,
ordering by mail is the surest route to coffee that is both well
selected and impeccably fresh.

CONSCIENTIOUS COFFEE STORAGE

Ideally, coffee is purchased weekly, like fresh-baked bread. You buy whole beans, store them in an airtight container at room temperature, and use them up.

The ideal, of course, isn't always practical. If you buy your coffee in small, sealed, one-way valve bags, you can keep these unopened at room temperature far longer. Once the seal is broken, however, the staling process begins.

When you buy coffee that has been exposed to air, or you open a one-way valve bag yourself, you can extend its staying power beyond two weeks by using this method: First, transfer whole-bean coffee to the smallest practical airtight container (a canning jar is ideal). Label the contents, and freeze them. Make sure the container you use is really airtight, and remember that the coffee bag doesn't qualify! Avoid plastic anything that may be tainted with other food tastes and odors; coffee soaks these up like a sponge.

For the same reason, avoid keeping coffee in the refrigerator. It is not cold enough to do much good and is invariably full of strongly scented foods. Beans should be used straight from the freezer, in manageable portions; avoid thawing and refreezing, which make the coffee wet and therefore stale. How long will these beans last? Frozen whole-bean coffee remains palatable for up to two months.

Just-in-Time Grinding

Except for using enough coffee (see "Proper Proportions" below), nothing will make a bigger difference in cup quality than buying whole beans and grinding them just before you brew. The punch behind the power of this statement is surface area: Coffee, once ground, has substantially more of it. After the bean's cellular structure is broken, oxidation and therefore (you guessed it) staling are accelerated exponentially. While whole-bean coffee is good for two weeks, the ground stuff is stale within hours.

The most extreme case, as usual, is typified by espresso: a single 7-gram dose of coffee, ground to the necessary exquisite fineness and spread so that the particles are touching but do not overlap, covers 3 square feet. This is the same space covered by a daily newspaper, laid open for perusal. Such a finely ground dose of coffee will stale irretrievably within an hour.

BLADE, BURR, AND HAND GRINDERS

So you need a grinder, but what kind? For any purpose other than professional-quality espresso, the small, cylindrical, whirring-blade "choppers" that sell for $20 or less work just fine. The greatest upgrade in taste will be had not by using a more sophisticated grinder but by using a grinder in the first place. Relative to the difference in taste between store-ground coffee and that ground right before brewing, making distinctions between grinders is just a parlor game.

A substantially more even grind does come from burr grinders, whose discs cut the beans into very precise pieces. One problem with the home versions, however, is the limited range of grind textures most produce. None of the electric models can accomplish the full range of grinds, from espresso to coarse. (This may be a moot point if you are wedded to one brewing method—in which case, make sure the grinder you buy can grind appropriately for it.) The other deterrent is cost; the Bunn burr grinder, clearly the best of all lower-priced units, sells for about $100 and grinds from cone filter to coarse. The best affordably priced unit is made by Braun. At around $55, it's probably the strongest all-around choice. The near-commercial-quality Jericho, at around $300, does everything well, but arguably requires the establishment of a small retail business to justify the investment in it!

Hand-powered grinders are an impractical choice for most, but for hard-core aficionados in search of the perfect particle the German-made Zassenhaus brand is worthy of consideration. This wood and steel grinder is lovely to look at and grinds the full range beautifully. But be warned: It will take you at least 15 minutes of cranking to turn out enough for one pot.

GRIND SIZE AND CONTACT TIME

For optimum flavor, coffee needs to be ground so that just the right amount of soluble material is extracted into the finished cup. If the grind is too fine, the water will take forever to make its way through. You will get overextracted, bitter-tasting coffee. Too coarse and the grounds and water hardly get to know one another; the brew will be underextracted, watery, and unsatisfying.

The right grind depends on how much time the coffee is going to take to brew. The more brief the contact time between grounds and water, the finer the grind should be. And vice versa: The longer the contact time, the coarser the grind. An espresso machine yields a shot of espresso in 20 seconds and so requires very finely ground coffee. A coffee

Grind Progression

Coffee press	Commercial drip brewer	Cone filter drip Vacuum pot	Home espresso machine
▼	▼	▼	▼
coarse	*medium*	*fine*	*very fine*

Home Grinding Guide

Brewing Method	Desired Grind	Brewing Time	Time in Blade Grinder
Saeco/Estro Home espresso machine	Very fine	20–25 seconds	25–30 seconds
Cone filter/ Vacuum pot	Fine	1–4 minutes	20–25 seconds
Commercial drip brewer	Medium	4–6 minutes	15 seconds
Plunger pot	Coarse	4–6 minutes	10 seconds

press, on the other hand, steeps the grounds in water for around 4 minutes. A coarse grind suits this method the best.

Good Water: 98 Percent of the Cup

Ninety-eight percent of every cup of coffee is water. The taste of the coffee, therefore, is directly related to the taste of the water used to brew it. For brewing, use fresh water free from any "off tastes" and odors. In a few lucky parts of the country, tap water is good enough to use as is. In most other instances, a simple carbon taste-and-odor filter is all that is required to produce the good water suitable for drinking and cooking.

Some mineral content ("hardness") in the water is actually desirable, as long as you bear in mind that the residual scale that builds up in your coffeemaking equipment will require more frequent cleaning. In some parts of the country, most notably southern California and Texas, excessive hardness and the presence of some other problems (sulfurous water, salt water intrusion, etc.) necessitate the use of bottled water. For brewing, avoid distilled or softened water, which won't properly extract flavor from the grounds.

When we say fresh water, we mean water that hasn't been sitting around for a long time. Water, just like anything else, will stale. As it stales, it loses oxygen, and this makes for flat, poorly extracted coffee.

The water you use should be not only good and fresh, but hot. In fact, *very* hot. The ideal temperature for all brewing methods other than espresso is 195–205°F, which is the same as "just-off-the-boil" at sea level. Achieving this exact temperature range is critically important to pulling good flavor into your coffee. As you will see, this requirement is particularly easy to meet when you boil water and brew manually. With home electric drip brewers, however, it becomes far more difficult to accomplish.

Proper Proportions: The Key to Good Coffee

With freshly roasted coffee and water suitable for brewing firmly in hand, it is time to brave the territory where more coffee-brewing mistakes are made than any other: the ratio of grounds to water.

The bottom line is that brewing great coffee requires adherence to one specific formula. Guessing and skimping don't work. It takes a little calculation to apply this formula to your own particular coffeemaker, but once achieved it can be effortlessly repeated. Get it down and you will have it for life.

As with good cooking, there is much to be learned from watching how professionals brew coffee. A good coffee bar or restaurant weighs each and every batch of ground coffee prior to brewing. Why? Individual coffees vary greatly in volume. For example, dark roasts are much less dense and contain less soluble material than lighter varieties. This is also true of many Indonesian coffees, and all decafs.

THE FORMULA

A standard restaurant pot is made by pouring a half-gallon (64 ounces) of water through a set weight of coffee. To make good coffee, this weight must be between 3.5 and 4.25 dry-weight ounces. Metrically speaking, this is 50–70 grams per liter. Less exact but easier for most of us to embrace is the measure in standard terms: a 1/4-pound per pot. (These days, the majority of restaurants outside the specialty realm use only half that amount—which may not be a bad thing, given the appalling quality of the coffee many buy.)

Do not be alarmed. We are *not* telling you to brew with a 1/4-pound of coffee every morning. The volumetric translation of this ratio is simple and far less imposing: 2 heaping tablespoons of coffee per 6 ounces of brewing water. Stay with us, and we will discuss this in more detail over the following pages.

If you do what most people do and skimp on coffee, your brew will be bitter. Some mistake this for stronger. After a few minutes on a burner, however, there's really no mistaking overextracted coffee; it tastes like paint thinner. What has happened is that instead of extracting the "middle" of the coffee—the desirable aromatic and flavor compounds—you extracted this *plus* all the coffee's bitter soluble components.

At the risk of sounding utterly technical, excellent-tasting coffee is achieved by extracting 18–22% of the weight of the grounds into the brew. There is a total of about 30 percent extractable material available, but the final 8 percent is made up entirely of bitter and otherwise undesirable flavor compounds.

So this is the chemistry behind the oft-repeated advice for varying the strength of coffee. First, use the basic equation to brew your coffee to recommended strength. If you then decide you want the coffee flavors to be less concentrated, dilute to taste with good, hot water.

The Basic Brewing Equation

 *Two heaping tablespoons of fresh, properly ground coffee*

+  *6 ounces of good, fresh water heated to just-off-the-boil (195°–205°F)*

+  *A brew time of 4–6 minutes*

 *One flavorful serving of fabulous coffee*

A NECESSARY DIGRESSION:
WHAT IS A "CUP" OF COFFEE?

The residential volumetric equivalent of the professional standard is 1 heaping standard coffee measure (2 tablespoons) per each 6 ounces of water poured through the grounds. Since the grounds absorb and retain water, this ratio results in a yield of about 5-1/2 fluid ounces.

This standard was developed decades ago, when fine china cups rather than gaping mugs were the norm. Quality, not quantity, was the priority. Coffee was brewed full-strength and tasted better; one hungered for less per sitting because it was so satisfying. Ergo smaller cups...

Throw out any odd-sized scoops you have, and buy a standard 2-tablespoon measure. Fill your coffeemaker with water, then determine its capacity by pouring the water into a measuring cup. Once you know the total number of ounces, divide it by 6. This will tell you how many 2-tablespoon measures you should use. For brewing, simply portion out this number with your new scoop. (But first, read "Drip Coffee" below to make sure your coffeemaker is capable of brewing full-strength without overflowing.)

Having established what a cup is, we can now determine how many of them 1 pound of coffee will make. The answer is 40 5-1/2–ounce servings of fabulously flavorful brew.

Make It Fresh, Drink It Fresh

Once brewed, drip coffee made with a filter should be held at 185–190°F. How long it will keep depends on where you keep it. On a warming plate or burner, brewed coffee retains

Common Coffee-Brewing Mistakes

If your coffee tastes "bitter":

- ▶ Too little coffee, too finely ground.

- ▶ Coffee was brewed with an overlong brewing cycle.

- ▶ Coffee was "cooked" on the burner or held too long after brewing.

If your coffee tastes "weak":

- ▶ Didn't use enough coffee (2 tablespoons of coffee per 6 ounces of brewing water).

- ▶ Coffee was too coarsely ground.

- ▶ Coffee was not brewed long enough (i.e., with a plunger pot, didn't wait long enough before plunging).

peak flavor for only about 20 minutes. Transferring coffee into a thermos or airpot—or brewing it straight into one in the first place—extends its useful life to 45–60 minutes.

But coffee stays hot much longer than that, we can hear you saying. Sure it does. However, oxidation and ongoing chemical reactions occurring in brewed coffee rapidly degrade its flavor. In a restaurant or coffee bar, an airpot without a timer attached to it displaying when the contents were brewed should inspire suspicion (the same freshness alarm that goes off when you see undated whole-bean coffee sitting in a bin). More frightening yet is the sight of a half-dozen airpots in a row at the "gourmet" store, each offering prebrewed—and prestaled—coffee for your convenience.

Brewed coffee that contains higher concentrations of oil and sediment, such as those brewed with a gold-washed filter, coffee press, or vacuum pot, should be consumed within 20 minutes. Because the fine particles and oils they contain continue brewing in the beverage, it serves little purpose to transfer them to a thermal container.

Brewing Methods: Finding the Best Fit

Our goal with this section is to steer people through the obstacle course that is brewing a great cup of coffee. We understand full well what it is like when the alarm goes off at 6:00 AM and you have to hit the road at 6:35, but you want a good, hot cup of coffee in your hand when you do. Chances are, you could be brewing coffee in a way that delivers flavors far superior to what you are getting now… in the same amount of time. Or less.

To decide which brewing method or methods best match your needs, start by asking yourself these questions:

1. On what occasions do I normally drink coffee? What is the relative importance of taste and convenience? (You may have more than one answer: for workday mornings vs. leisurely entertaining, for example.)

2. How much money am I willing to spend on brewing equipment? On coffee?

3. Can this brewing method brew great-tasting coffee?

For most coffee drinkers, the biggest hurdle to overcome as you begin getting serious about coffee is the fact that you own an electric drip coffeemaker, and the vast majority of electric drip brewers sacrifice taste for convenience. What we humbly suggest, if good taste is your goal, is an investment of attention rather than dollars. Grinding fresh and measuring coffee precisely becomes second nature after a week. If you are going to the trouble of sourcing fresh, optimally roasted beans, brew to capture every precious nuance of flavor and aroma you're paying for.

We define great brewing methods as those that meet all the criteria, the "essential elements," we have just discussed for brewing a great cup. (Remember that your familiarity with the essential elements of great coffee gives you the tools to evaluate any brewing method, too.) There are several great methods that, while a bit more "hands-on" than automatic methods, brew monumentally better coffee in considerably less time. These manual brewers are also simple, easy to use and maintain, and inexpensive.

Over the following pages, we will focus on three brewing methods that offer the highest possible cup quality:

the manual drip coffee maker, the coffee press or plunger pot, and the vacuum pot.

DRIP COFFEE

Great drip coffee combines the essential brewing elements in a very specific way. You need a filter that contains a heaping measure of fresh grounds for each 6 ounces of brewer capacity, and water heated to 195–205°F. The water should saturate the grounds thoroughly and gently; the total brew cycle, start to finish, must take 4–6 minutes. If it takes more than 8 minutes, the coffee will be overextracted.

This sounds relatively simple, and is—as long as you are brewing coffee by hand, in a manual drip maker. (It is also relatively easy to accomplish if your kitchen is equipped with a $1,000, plumbed-in commercial brewer, but that's a different story.) It is all but impossible to brew drip coffee that meets the above criteria using typical home electric brewers, and herein lies the source of the frustration so many coffee lovers encounter when they try to duplicate good coffee-bar coffee at home.

"Automatic drip" brewers are exactly what their name suggests: an attempt to automate something that was originally done by hand. By taking a detailed look at the process you are trying to automate, it becomes much easier to understand why most home electric brewers make such poor coffee. For this run-through, we will use the specific manual drip setup we rate as the best. However, similar effects can be achieved with other brands and components.

Our Manual Drip Method

To brew manual drip coffee, we start by bringing a quart of fresh, cold water to a boil. The easiest way to do this is to use an electric kettle, which heats water much faster than a burner or microwave. The inexpensive Rival brand kettle we use happens to have a 1-quart capacity, which matches the container we brew into precisely; many other brands have similarly convenient markings. While the water heats, we assemble the brewer and grind our beans.

We brew directly into a quart-size Nissan thermos using a matching filter cone (made by the same company). This thermos is made entirely of stainless steel and insulates with a vacuum layer, so there's no fragile glass liner. The filter cone is made to use a #4 size paper filter, but we cheat a bit and upgrade to a #6. This provides a little extra height for the grounds to expand as the water first moistens them. The additional room is invaluable when brewing recently roasted or especially low-density coffees, which froth and swell significantly during brewing. The entire cone/thermos combination costs about $45.

Grinding and measuring are also made easy by choosing this particular size. Our very typical blade grinder contains about 2 ounces of coffee when filled to capacity—perfect for the 1-quart "pot" we're preparing. Because the coffee brews in about 4 minutes, we grind our beans for 25 seconds and dump them in the filter cone.

When the water has reached a boil, the kettle whistles. We pause for a beat to achieve the just-off-boil temperature range, then wet the grounds with water. They quickly rise to form a cap. After a few seconds, the cap settles, and we pour more water over the grounds. Each time the water level in the filter lowers, we pour more—until our kettle is completely empty. Sure enough, the pouring process lasts about 4 minutes. Our fragrant, steaming, and delicious pot of coffee is done.

Manual Drip Brewing

This method is the original version of what electric home brewers have long sought to imitate. Ground coffee is measured into a filter placed atop an insulated container, and water is poured over the coffee so that the brew "drips" right into the thermos.

Amount of Coffee: For a 1-quart thermos, use 1 quart of freshly boiled water and 2 dry-weight ounces (.12 on a digital scale) of beans. A good volumetric approximation for this amount is a 12-ounce paper cup filled 3/4-full, or a blade grinder's worth.

Grind: Medium; about 20–25 seconds in a blade grinder.

Steps for Brewing:

1. Put a kettle's worth of good, fresh water on the stove to boil (or, if the kettle is electric, plug it in).

2. If using a paper filter, rinse and place it in the filter holder atop the thermos. (Hint: Use a paper filter one size larger than the holder calls for.)

3. Grind the coffee and place it in the paper (or gold-washed) filter.

4. Once your water has reached the boiling point, remove it from heat. Pause for a moment, then pour it to wet the grounds. Fill the filter with water each time the level drops, continuing until all of the water has been poured through the grounds.

5. Remove the filter, pour yourself a cup of hot coffee, and cap the thermos—but only until you find yourself ready for another cup.

Manual vs. Automatic Drip

In our extensive testing of home automatic brewers, no model under $150 came close to producing coffee of the quality we brewed with our manual method. Even the best commercial units do no better. Why is this so?

Using the manual method, we bring all the water to the correct temperature before brewing. The physics of heating with residential wattage make this all but impossible for most home electric coffeemakers—especially when a large part of the available juice is dedicated to heating the burners that are supposed to keep brewed coffee hot. Most units can't get water above the mid-180°F range, which is nowhere near hot enough for optimum flavor extraction.

Next, our open-top cone and oversized filter let us use the proper amount of coffee. Virtually no home electric brewer holds close to the correct amount. Even upscale models cater to mass-market preferences: a weak pot, with stale coffee (so no degassing is expected). To obtain decent results, you have to "short" the pot—use less water—or start cleaning when the messy grounds overflow.

Finally, our brewing process takes 4 minutes. *A typical electric unit takes 11 or 12 minutes.* When the grounds and water stay in contact for more than 8 minutes, the result is overextraction; as you know, the coffee will be bitter. Commercial drip brewers meet the critical 195–205°F temperature and 4–6 minute brew cycle requirements, but home electrics don't. This, in a nutshell, is why you can't make "professional" coffee using one of these machines.

With all the bells and whistles coffeemakers boast, why are the fundamentals so poorly attended to? We asked this question of a designer responsible for many of the best-selling home electric models.

"This is a volume business," he replied, "we sell thousands and thousands of each design. The criteria are simple: They have to sell—profitably—for $49.95 or less. We build them to be thrown out within eighteen months of purchase, because that's what lots of people do; they throw these out rather than giving them a good cleaning.

"Besides, the machines work just fine according to *Consumer Reports*. But don't ask me. I don't drink coffee."

If you love great drip coffee (as we do), the biggest favor you can do yourself is to unplug your electric model and brew by hand. At present, there is just one alternative: the Dutch-made Technivorm, which is the only home electric that brews to professional standards. These makers start at about $150. They aren't cheap, but when you weigh their ability to brew excellent coffee over decades against replacing a less expensive brewer every few years and suffering through mediocre coffee all the while, you may conclude that the investment is worthwhile.

For those who are really willing to compromise, we will relent slightly and mention two other models. The Rowenta thermos brewer (about $75) is capable of brewing a decent cup, providing the roast is relatively light (darker roasts and super-fresh light ones will overflow the brew basket). The brew temperature is only a few degrees short of ideal, and the glass-lined carafe does a good job of retaining heat and aroma. Brew time is over 8 minutes, so adjust by using a medium- rather than fine-cone filter grind.

The Bunn Home Brewer, which is widely available through discount retailers for just under $50, comes closer to duplicating commercial machine performance than any of the upscale department store brands. Its brew cycle is actually too short (3-1/2 minutes) and it won't hold a full dose of fresh coffee. But if you cut the water to a quart and use a rather fine drip grind, you end up with decent drip coffee. Because the Bunn brews into a glass pot on a burner, you need to drink the finished coffee right after brewing.

On Filters

The advantage of using paper filters is the complete clarity of the finished brew. Its body is relatively light, and the coffee remains palatable longer than that of any other method. We recommend the "oxygen-whitened" (non-chlorine-bleached) variety; bleaching is an environmental no-no, while brown, unbleached filters can impart a woody taste to the brew. You can reduce the paper taste of any filter by rinsing it with a little good water before you fill it with ground coffee.

Gold-washed filters have the great advantage of lasting for months, even years, if gently hand-washed. These filters are made of fine mesh lightly coated with gold, which prevents coffee oils from clinging better than any other metal. Gold-washed filters leave a higher concentration of sediment and flavorful oils in the finished brew; the coffee is slightly more intense, the pot life somewhat shorter. We find these trade-offs worthwhile—besides, the grounds easily emptied from these filters make great compost.

THE COFFEE PRESS

Many people have seen a coffee press, but it's astonishing how few have actually used one—and how impressed coffee lovers are, once they try the coffee pouring out, with its taste. The coffee press, or plunger pot, is simple, elegant, and hands-down the easiest way to make good coffee. Pour

Brewing Coffee in a Coffee Press

This simple, elegant brewer is the easiest way to make good coffee. Freshly boiled water is poured over coarsely ground coffee, then allowed to infuse for about four minutes. The plunger's stainless steel filter is then pressed down through the infusion, resulting in a very thickly textured cup rich in natural coffee oils.

Amount of Coffee: Bodum, the principal manufacturer of these and many other brewers, defines a "cup" as 4 ounces. The 1-cup scoop which comes with their products is sized accordingly, holding 7 grams of medium-roasted coffee. For the most popular 1-liter ("8-cup") size, use 2 dry weight ounces of beans (.12 on a digital scale). A convenient volumetric approximation for this amount is a 12-ounce paper cup filled 3/4-full, or a blade grinder's worth.

Grind: Coarse, about 12 seconds in a blade grinder.

Steps for Brewing:
1. Make sure the brewer is clean. If it has been sitting unused for any length of time, residual oils in the filter screen assembly may be rancid and will spoil anything you brew. To avoid this common problem, disassemble the screen, scrub it thoroughly by hand with dish soap, clean, and reassemble. Always store your plunger pot with a couple of inches of water covering the screens; coffee oils only turn rancid when they dry.

2. Measure your ground coffee into the press pot, and bring a liter of fresh water to boil in a kettle.

3. Remove your kettle from the heat, wait a moment to achieve the just-off-boil temperature, and pour half the water over the grounds. Give them a quick stir, add the rest of the water and place the filter assembly loosely on top. (This traps the aroma.)

4. Enter 4 minutes on your countdown timer and press start, or keep a close eye on your watch.

5. When the 4 minutes are up, gently press the plunger through the grounds and serve. If you encounter much resistance when you start to plunge, pull up gently on the plunger and then continue pressing down. Always press straight down, not at an angle, to avoid breaking the glass.

To brew iced coffee:

1. Grind and measure twice the amount of coffee used for coffee served hot.

2. Follow steps 2–5 above. As the coffee brews, fill serving cups or a pitcher full to the top with ice (made from good water, of course). You may encounter extra resistance when plunging.

3. Pour the double-strength coffee over the ice. Enjoy!

The best coffees to serve iced fall into two camps: those with strong floral or fruity tastes, such as Kenya, and those with milder characteristics. Here's an unusual must-try: half Sumatra, half French. Mind-bogglingly strong when hot, this combination has great presence and persistence when diluted over ice.

fresh boiled water over medium to coarsely ground coffee, then allow it to infuse for about four minutes. Press the plunger's stainless steel filter down through the infusion, and you get a very thickly textured cup that is full of natural coffee oils.

The sediment produced with the coffee press is an acquired taste for some. The modest pressure you use to plunge at the tail end of brewing accentuates the perceived acidity of a coffee, making this an especially good choice for low-acid Indonesians and darker blends. Pressing, incidentally, is the most flavorful way to brew decaf. Once you try it, you will never go back.

Coffee-press coffee should be consumed within 20 minutes of preparation. Because the oils and particles in the finished brew continue to extract even after plunging, decanting the contents of a coffee press into a thermos for longer storage is not recommended.

THE VACUUM POT

Few people these days have even seen, let alone used, a vacuum pot. Vacuum-pot brewing represents the ideal for which drip brewing is a convenience-oriented compromise. The setup looks a bit unwieldy and quite fragile, but it was the method of choice in diners and restaurants across the country through the early 1950s. Today, vacuum pots are found mainly in high-end Japanese coffee houses and at home with in-the-know coffee connoisseurs.

The brewer looks something like an hourglass. Water comes to a boil in the bottom bowl, while the grounds sit in the top. The boiling action pushes the water upstairs to mix with the grounds, where it infuses at just-below-boiling

Brewing Coffee in a Vacuum Pot

Invented in 1840 by Scottish engineer Robert Napier, this brewer is one way to reach the subtler flavors of truly fine coffee. It has two glass or metal globes that fit together to make a seal. A plug, often attached to a spring, seats in the upper globe. Before assembling, make sure both globes are clean and free from coffee oils or debris.

Amount of Coffee: The Bodum Santos is the preferred model—affordably priced and high-quality—and it holds 1 liter. Use 2 dry-weight ounces of beans (.12 on a digital scale). An easy approximation for this amount is a 12-ounce paper cup filled 3/4-full, or a blade grinder's worth.

Grind: Fine, 20–25 seconds in a blade grinder. The grind for a vacuum pot is the same as for drip coffee.

Steps for Brewing:

1. Fill the lower chamber 3/4-full with fresh water.

2. Install the filter, plug, or spring device in the top globe. Measure the proper amount of coffee into the top globe and fit it to the bottom globe so a seal is made between the two.

3. Place the assembled pot over medium-high heat.

4. When the water heats to brew temperature, it will ascend into the upper chamber. Stir the hot water into the coffee and lower the heat.

5. When almost all of the water is in the upper globe, begin timing. Any water remaining in the lower

globe will bubble slightly, keeping the liquid in the top globe. At the end of 3 minutes, remove the pot from the heat or turn off the flame.

6. When the heat source is removed, a vacuum will develop in the lower globe as it cools. Brewed coffee will flow into the lower chamber, leaving spent grounds in the top.

7. When all coffee has descended into the lower globe, the coffee will gurgle slightly. Remove the top globe and serve.

temperatures for three minutes. You must then move the whole thing away from the heat, at which point a vacuum develops in the lower bowl as a result of its slight cooling.

This vacuum draws the brewed coffee down. Once it's all there, get ready to enjoy it. Like drip coffee, the finished brew is almost perfectly clear—but with absolutely no influence from paper filters. It also pours out piping hot, more so than coffee made by any other method. The entire process takes about six minutes after the water is hot, and once underway needs no tending beyond a watchful eye.

In the words of food expert Corby Kummer, the vacuum pot is truly "the CD player of coffeemakers: all you taste is the coffee." Because of its fragility and seemingly cumbersome nature, the vacuum pot is probably destined to occasional or weekend use, at least by all but the most hard-core consumers. But if you cherish coffees that are bright or aromatically complex, or never can seem to get your coffee hot enough, you may find a vacuum brewer to be a very rewarding investment.

MISCELLANEOUS METHODS

Flip-Drip or Neapolitan

This oddly shaped brewer is made up of two little pots joined in the middle by a two-sided strainer. You heat water in one side of the pot, then flip the whole apparatus over—whereupon the coffee drips through the strainer into the empty side. These are fun little jobs, but most are made of aluminum, which is not desirable for coffeemakers (coffee oils eat away at the metal—not particularly good for your health or the brewer's). The cup style is similar to, but invariably cooler than, manual drip brewed with a gold-washed filter right into a thermos.

Cold-Water Concentrate

This brewing method is offered by two manufacturers, Filtron and Toddy. To brew cold-water coffee, you use the coffee maker to steep a pound of coffee overnight, then filter the result through nylon mesh disks. The resulting concentrate must be stored in the refrigerator, and keeps well for a week or two. Hot coffee is made by mixing small amounts of the concentrate with hot water, cold coffee by mixing with cold water.

Cold-water brewers are marketed as being ideal for those in search of "low-acid" coffee, and they do remove some of the slight acidity coffee possesses. Since all coffee is low in acidity, however, "low-acid" in this case seems to be used as the equivalent of "mild."

Because cold water doesn't extract much flavor from coffee, the best way to get a flavorful extract is to use a blend with more kick than you might seek otherwise. One ferocious-sounding favorite is half Sumatra and half French roast; out of a cold-water brewer, this tastes pretty middle-of-the-road. Another good choice is a straight Ethiopian Harrar or, if you're feeling flush, Yemen Mocha; their fruity high notes come through surprisingly well. Relative to the instant coffee that comes from a jar, "instant" cold water coffee is manna from heaven. Compared to great coffee brewed with hot water, however, it's just instant coffee.

Middle Eastern Coffee

Aficionados of this ancient brewing method are probably the only coffee drinkers who would characterize straight espresso as being a bit too mild or lacking in body! To make it properly, you need the right tools: a conical copper or brass pot known as an *ibrik*, a special grinder that looks like—and is occasionally sold as—a pepper mill, and the smallest demitasse cups you can find.

The coffee must be freshly ground and needs to be powder fine. Blade grinders won't do the job, and neither will most commercial units. Use the pepper mill type, or a mortar, pestle, and lots of elbow grease.

The ibrik should be filled less than half full in order to allow enough room for the coffee to froth and expand. Figure proportions by measuring 2 teaspoons of grounds and 1 of sugar per demitasse of water; you can adjust the amount of sugar to taste over time. Since this method involves boiling and drinking the grounds, a substantial amount of sugar is used to keep bitterness in check. Cardamom is often added as well, ground with the coffee at a casual ratio of one seed (*seed,* not pod) per demitasse.

Bring the mixture to a boil over medium heat, then reduce the heat to low and watch the coffee carefully as it boils. When the foam reaches the top of the ibrik's narrow neck and overflow seems imminent, turn off the heat and fill each demitasse halfway with coffee. Then return to each and top off with foam. The end result, once you get the hang of it, is a thimbleful of supremely flavorful elixir.

Trade Secrets for Superlative Coffee

BENCHMARKING COFFEE BY THE CUP

Walk into any specialty coffee store that you know pays knowledgeable and consistent attention to its brewing, and taste the coffee. It's good, and that is no accident. The very costly machinery is capable of brewing at the recommended temperatures and runs an accurate, 4-minute brewing cycle. The shop uses a seemingly large amount of coffee relative to the size of the filter, so paper tastes are diffused.

With the taste you experience fixed firmly on your palate, go home and experiment with some of the techniques we outline in this chapter.

ADJUSTING BREW STRENGTH

If you want a milder cup of coffee than the formula yields, don't get to it by skimping on coffee. Chances are, you will end up with an underextracted brew, which may be milder but will not represent a balanced, pleasing range of coffee flavors. Instead, brew at full strength and then dilute the resulting coffee with fresh, hot water. This way, you will be using the formula that brings you the best flavor, then moderating its concentration in the way you find satisfying.

MATCHING COFFEES WITH BREWING METHODS

Each of the preferred brewing methods results in a dramatically different finished cup style, highlighting some aspects of a given coffee's character while pushing others into the background. Just as there is a strong and unequivocal relationship between the brewing method you use and the roast style you enjoy, so there is a relationship between your brewing method and the kinds of coffee you like best. Matching coffee type and degree of roast to brewing method may sound rather esoteric, but it is really a lot of fun. We promise: Your guests will be amazed. Here are a few generalizations to get you started.

Manual Drip

The drip method is like a muted version of vacuum-pot coffee; the muting comes mostly from the paper filter, which absorbs and retains some aromatic compounds. This method yields a cup that is light in body, and well suited for early in the day. A coffee that tastes a bit too acidic and light in a plunger pot will "resolve" as perfectly brewed drip. *Classic experiences:* Costa Rican Dota or La Minita, Guatemalan Antigua, Kenya, Ethiopian Yergacheffe, and other coffees that possess subtle flavors.

Coffee Press

The coffee press highlights body over aroma and varietal nuance. Because of the slight pressure exerted on the coffee during brewing, the perceived acidity of a given coffee increases slightly. This method is a beautiful match for medium-roasted Latin American and East African coffees and is perfect above all for brewing the Indonesians, whose lush body and relatively low acidity seem to exist precisely for this purpose. *Classic experiences:* Sumatra, Sulawesi, Yemen Mocha, Ethiopian Harrar, darker roasts of any of the great Latin American or East Africans, and any good decaffeinated coffee.

Vacuum Pot

The vacuum pot highlights aroma, acidity, and country-of-origin flavors, while keeping body relatively light. It is ideal for light to medium-roasted Latin American and East African coffees. Classic experiences: Costa Rican Dota or La Minita, Guatemalan Antigua, Kenya, Ethiopian Yerga-cheffe, and other coffees that possess subtle flavors.

C H A P T E R   8

Espresso: A World unto Itself

You're perched in the window seat of your favorite café, watching the world walk by and sipping an ethereal and absolutely delicious cappuccino. You raise the porcelain bowl to your lips and take in velvety smooth milk, full and soft and comforting. Espresso streams through, and when the concentrated heat of it reaches your tongue the flavors are spicy, bittersweet-chocolate-and-caramel-like, rich, and assertive. There is nothing else like it.

What does it take to duplicate this experience? Well, in order to duplicate it, you have to know what it took to create this exquisite beverage in the first place.

No matter what espresso drink you order, the beverage includes at least one ounce-sized shot of espresso. To brew that shot of espresso, your *barista* (Italian for "bartender") has to do the following, and rapidly: Tamp down 7 grams of extremely finely ground coffee with a force of approximately 50 psi; pull an ounce of good, fresh, hot (192°F–198°F) water through the coffee with a force of about 130 psi; make sure that happened over a span of 18–24 seconds; then get the resulting shot in your drink and to you *pronto.*

Brewing espresso is not simply pouring hot water through ground coffee. Unlike other methods of brewing coffee, this *is* rocket science. True espresso is uniquely a product of technology...it is about machinery. To avoid disappointment when attempting to replicate the experience at home, this must be understood.

Espresso is to all other brewing methods what an electron microscope is to a magnifying glass. Everything that figures into brewing "regular" coffee—coffee type, degree of roast, coffee freshness, grind, water, contact time, temperature, holding time—matters exponentially more with espresso. And although it is a product of technology, the mentality that machines, not people, make coffee (which, as we have already seen, causes gargantuan problems with something as simple as a pot of drip), won't work at all with this brewing method. Here, the skill and care of the operator are paramount.

When You Brew Espresso at Home...

Consider the two distinct ways Italians enjoy their coffee. At home, most brew not espresso but simple, strong coffee in a macchinetta—an inexpensive stovetop maker. For espresso, on the other hand, they head down the street to their neighborhood coffee bar. There, a seasoned barista with at least $7,500 worth of espresso machine, grinder, and fresh coffee at his disposal makes them a perfect *caffè*. Homemade coffee is good but espresso is great, and no one confuses the two. In a sense, both are coffee, but only in the same way that the Fiat mini in the carport and the boss's Ferrari are both cars.

Our expectations of espresso, like those of consumers in its native land, are based on the experience we enjoy at the hands of professionals operating powerful commercial equipment. To approach this standard, we must possess a smaller version capable of generating similar water temperature and pressure.

There are scores of home machines out there, but it requires a substantial investment of money and time to make true, straight espresso happen at home. The more money you are willing to pay, the closer to the commercial standard you will come. No one wants to hear this, but it's true: The home espresso machines you see that fall within a certain price range, particularly those that fall at or below $100, are going to disappoint you. Period.

If, on the other hand, it is the soothing stimulation of frothed milk layered over strong, rich coffee that drives you to pursue espresso, you have a few more options. You can even achieve excellent results using simple equipment that looks—and costs!—nothing like professional gear. As we will explain, a coffee press paired with a separate milk steamer is a versatile and effective duo that yields far better coffee than most entry-level espresso machines.

Before you shell out a substantial sum for home espresso equipment, we encourage you to gain at least a few minutes of personal experience with a "gold standard": a professional machine and grinder. In an espresso bar, these function so inseparably they may as well be one entity.

Don't expect to be greeted with open arms everywhere when seeking this experiment (or, for that matter, *anywhere* during a morning rush). But if at all possible, find yourself a coffee store that sells both espresso beverages and home machines. Smile big, then arrange to pull a shot or two on their commercial machine during a slow period. Note the size and heft of the machine, and pay particular attention to the heavy, heat-retaining metal from which the portafilter, which holds ground coffee for brewing, is fashioned. With this experience in hand, you will be much better equipped to evaluate home models.

We advocate purchasing home espresso machines from this type of store. Chances are, one or more staff members have already tested every model and will be happy to share their unvarnished opinions. They will also be more willing to offer demonstrations and tutorials, and help with fine-tuning as you progress through the learning curve at home.

There are entire books written on espresso and how to brew it. If you are seriously interested in perfecting this method in either a home or retail setting, we recommend that you invest in one or more of them. In this chapter, we will take a closer look at each of the components of good espresso as they relate to the larger realm of specialty coffee, and discuss several affordable methods for brewing satisfying espresso at home.

Understanding the Four Italian "M"s

All things having to do with art, soul, and physical pleasure—especially in the culinary category—bloom under Italian hands. Espresso is a case in point. The Italians have been brewing espresso for almost a hundred years, and where preparation is concerned they hold the patent on perfection. According to them, the conditions necessary for brewing proper espresso can be summed up by four "M"s:

1. *Macinazione* (ma-chee-na-tzee-*oh*-nay): the correct grinding of the coffee blend.

2. *Miscela* (mee-*shay*-la): the coffee blend.

3. *Macchina* (*mah*-kee-nah): the espresso machine.

4. *Mano* (*mah*-no): the skilled "hand" of the operator, or barista.

These are the essential elements for brewing good espresso in any venue. Use them as criteria for evaluating home brewing methods—or any retail operation you patronize, for that matter—to discern whether or not the combination in use is a viable one.

MACINAZIONE: GRIND AND GRINDER

The barista grinds your coffee using a powerful and exacting burr grinder, reducing the coffee to almost microscopic fineness. Coffee particles ground for brewing on a good espresso machine are so minute that the amount needed for a 1-ounce serving, 7 grams, will inhabit the space of an unfolded daily newspaper. That's stretching approximately 2 full tablespoons into the space of 3 square feet.

The quality of the flow of espresso, or "pour," is a function of several interrelated factors: grind, ambient humidity and temperature, specific coffee blend, and the amount of pressure exerted by the barista when tamping the grounds before brewing. In a good espresso bar, the fineness of the grind is tuned subtly every few hours in response to changes in atmosphere and personnel. More than any other brewing method, freshness is crucial here. Coffee for expresso should be ground within one hour of, and preferably just before, use. The rapidity of staling—which results from the increased exposure to air via a larger surface area—means that it is impossible to brew excellent espresso at home without grinding the coffee fresh yourself.

The only type of grinder capable of such fineness and the necessary consistency is a near-commercial-quality burr grinder (see Appendix B). If you decide to invest in one of the $500-plus home espresso machines, you will need to add one of these pricey numbers to your shopping list as well. Unfortunately, those valiant little blade grinders will never be able to grind coffee finely enough for a high-end home espresso machine—at least not without generating a great deal of heat, which spoils flavor by releasing precious aromatics prematurely. (*Exception:* Blade grinders can be used successfully with the Saeco/Estro espresso machines. For a full discussion, keep reading.)

MISCELA: THE COFFEE BLEND

Great espresso blends are function-specific. Brewed by any other means, a great espresso blend will taste somewhat bland and simple. But through the espresso machine, this coffee will express stunning aromatic intensity, balanced and subtle flavors, and an aftertaste that lingers for minutes.

Good espresso blends are low in acidity. The espresso method's high-pressure mode of extraction greatly enhances perceived acidity in the finished shot, so a little acidity goes a surprisingly long way. The lower level of acidity desired—and really required—for an espresso blend can be achieved through careful selection of component coffees, changes to their degree of roast, or both.

A fine northern Italian espresso blend often uses Brazilian coffee, which is nutty and low-acid, as its base component. Flavor complexity is added through the incorporation of other Latin American coffees. The roast is in the Vienna roast range, showing slight to moderate oil on the bean surface—dark compared to American canned coffee but far lighter than the average roast of most specialty coffees in the United States.

Most Italian roasters add robusta coffee, which puts a rough note in the flavor but also contributes to the density of the espresso's *crema* because of its high concentration of oils. Such impressive density can be achieved without robusta, and several of the best Italian roasters, including the internationally renowned Illycaffè of Trieste, produce superb espresso without resorting to use of this species.

There's a tremendous diversity of imported Italian and domestic Italian-style espresso blends available in the United States, some of the best—and freshest—of which are produced by American roasters. Relative to the other major style of espresso discussed below, these blends are mild and delicate; they have good body, but the focus is on aroma and flavor. The most traditional are formulated not for how they will taste with milk, which is only an incidental concern for most Italians, but for how they will taste when combined with a teaspoon of sugar, which is how Italians drink espresso more than 90 percent of the time.

The artistry that goes into the best of these blends is truly impressive. For example, Carlo Di Ruocco of Mr.

Espresso in Oakland, California, routinely roasts a dozen or more top-quality straight coffees, then blends them precisely in order to achieve the layered complexity and subtlety that is artisan Italian espresso at its best.

Some American roasters are ignorant to the intricacies of the development of the espresso tradition, and unequivocally recommend their darkest roast for brewing. This results in an undrinkably bitter brew. On the other hand, there is a rich American espresso tradition that, while fully cognizant and appreciative of Italian approaches, has chosen a different path. Roasters who are part of this movement employ aristocratic, high-grown Latin American and Indonesian coffees with much higher inherent acidity and flavor intensity than those used in most Italian blends. They roast the beans dark enough to corral their acidity, but not so much so that they veer off into roasty bitterness. The best of these blends yield very dense, sweet, big espresso—large-scale Barolo, not light and fruity Beaujolais.

This practice was initiated and perfected by Starbucks Coffee Company founder and current owner of Peet's Coffee in San Francisco, Jerry Baldwin, and has since been popularized by several other high-quality roasters. Espresso of this sort has great power and presence both by itself and in milk—no sugar necessary!

While we are confident you will find a well-crafted blend to be the best choice for daily espresso brewing, there are numerous straight coffees that yield memorable espresso experiences. Espresso distills a coffee to its very essence, affording a unique glimpse of the bean's core personality.

Avoid very light as well as the very darkest roasts (such as French). As espresso, these taste respectively like lemonade and creosote. Moderately dark roasts of the following coffees are particularly worth trying: Guatemalan Antigua, Ethiopian Sidamo or Yergacheffe, Kenya, Yemen Mocha, Estate Java, Sumatra, and Sulawesi.

MACCHINA: THE ESPRESSO MACHINE

The crucial ingredients here are pressure, or brewing force, and temperature control. They constitute the real stumbling blocks to successful espresso brewing at home; it takes a sophisticated and powerful machine to provide them.

To brew true espresso, the brewing water has to come through extremely fine coffee at 9 atmospheres of pressure, or 130 psi. If it isn't brewed at this pressure, it isn't espresso—it is only double-strength coffee. The pressure is requisite for releasing the unique tastes and thick, sweet, abundant crema of a good shot of espresso. You may grow to love the taste of coffee brewed on a Neapolitan or other double-strength maker, but it won't be true espresso, and can't match the taste of a well-prepared shot from a commercial machine.

The challenge to the machine is made more difficult by the fact that to steam milk, water must be raised to over 212°F. To brew, the water must be delivered within the narrow temperature range of 192°F–198°F. It takes power to generate this heat, and precise control to balance it. This isn't easy for commercial equipment; a thermostat for the one type of commercial machine that does it well costs about $300—more than most home machines. So what does this mean for the home barista? In many cases, short-lived steaming pressure and severely scorched coffee.

Most consumers assume that the name, "home espresso machine," indicates that even the models under $100 are equal to their task. This is a very logical conclusion—and frustrations quickly arise when consumers try to duplicate the experience they have in a store. These creatures are difficult and time-consuming to use, brew disappointing shots, and are an utter mess to clean. More than any other piece of kitchen equipment, the low-cost, steam-driven, multi-function home espresso machines end up as garage clutter or yard sale inventory.

Even the majority of the machines under $200 are steam-driven, so they can't regulate temperature accurately enough and the pressure isn't nearly what is required for brewing espresso. These machines, too, yield a burnt-tasting and typically overextracted double-strength coffee.

The home versions of true espresso machines, characterized by powerful pumps and sturdy, industrial-grade heating elements, start at around $250. They approach commercial heft and durability at double or triple that price. Excellent results are obtainable on many of these, providing the operator knows what good espresso looks, smells, and tastes like, and is patient and willing to practice.

We make the assumption that, like us, the majority of our readers are as concerned about price as they are eager to make good espresso at home. For that reason, the specific brewing apparatuses we recommend are the two options under $300 that we feel duplicate the experience of well prepared coffee-bar espresso, or at least something pleasingly close to it, at home. Here they are.

Saeco (Estro)

This machine, marketed as Estro by Starbucks Coffee Company, rings in at around $260 (sometimes as low as $160 on sale). It has quite a strong little pump motor and

Brewing Home Espresso

With a strong pump and its ground-breaking adjustable portafilter, the Saeco/Estro is by far the best affordable home espresso machine. Making espresso with this machine is fairly easy to master, and the results are superb.

Dosage: The machine comes with two portafilter inserts, a "single" (for one 1-ounce serving) and a "double" (for two). Fill whichever insert you're using all the way to the top, but do not pack or tamp. For reference: the double takes just less than two full coffee measures, the single just less than one.

Grind: Herein lies the beauty of this machine. The portafilter adjusts to almost any degree of fineness a blade grinder can produce. For best results, grind in the neighborhood of fine to very fine, or 20–30 seconds.

Steps for Brewing:
1. Prime the machine by turning it on and running water through both the steam wand and the portafilter mount. This is very important for the health of the machine. Make sure the portafilter is tightened into the machine so it heats appropriately. If you want to steam milk, press the steam button. Wait for the green ready light.

2. Sink the steam wand into your pitcher of cold milk, then activate the steam knob on the side of the machine. When you are done, turn off the flow and take the milk from the wand. Clean the wand with a clean, wet rag and a few short steam bursts.

3. Deactivate the steam button, and wait for the ready light to come on again. As you are waiting, spoon ground coffee into your portafilter, making it level with the top of the insert. Once the ready light is on, tighten the portafilter up into the machine, pulling its handle all the way to your right. Place your shot glass(es) under the portafilter.

4. Activate the brew button on the front panel of the machine. Because the valve at the bottom of the filter is closed, nothing will come out. Listen attentively to the sound of the pump.

5. After about 3 seconds, or as soon as the motor's pitch drops, slowly bring the portafilter handle back to the left. The espresso will begin to flow; regulate the pour rate by adjusting the handle minutely.

6. When your shot glass(es) are filled to the 1-ounce line, close the valve by returning the handle to the right. *Immediately* deactivate the brew button. Add the shots to your drink, and enjoy.

7. As soon as possible afterward, release any pressure in the portafilter by swinging the handle slowly to the left, then removing it from the machine.Clean all parts thoroughly.

We recommend backflushing, or "brewing" without coffee in the portafilter, after each session with the machine. Backflush by pushing the handle from left to right several times while the brew water is activated. This helps to clear old coffee grounds from the portafilter mount, keeping the taste of your coffee unadulterated by residue.

one ground-breaking feature: an adjustable portafilter. Grind accuracy is not as crucial here as elsewhere because the portafilter itself, within a certain window, will automatically adjust to the character of the grounds.

You don't have to tamp the coffee. Just level it off and tighten the portafilter up into the machine, pulling its handle all the way to the right. This way, when you activate the flow of brewing water the valve at the bottom of the filter will stay closed. At first, the noise of the pump is alarmingly loud and cantankerous; it is driving water to saturate the grounds and build pressure inside the basket.

After about three seconds, or as soon as the initial racket subsides, slowly open the valve by bringing the portafilter handle back to the left. (We actually open it only to the point at which the caramel-striped color and undulating body of the pour match our expectations. The flow rate should be languid, like honey dripping off a spoon.)

When your shot glasses are appropriately full, swiftly close the valve by turning the handle to the right. Deactivate the water flow immediately. Espresso from this machine is superb, the brewing process easy to refine—especially compared to other machines in this price category. The steaming function is admirably consistent and fairly long-lived, making the Saeco a good option for entertaining.

Coffee Press and Milk Steamer

In North America, 95 percent of people who try making espresso at home are after the *latte* experience. You can create a tremendously satisfying and intense espresso-style beverage using equipment that does not fit into the traditional espresso category at all. For the investment of time and money that one is willing to make, a coffee press and stand-alone milk steamer will deliver a dramatically more pleasing experience. No, it won't look as espresso-like as the $150 machine sitting on your kitchen counter. But please, educate your friends to get beyond this. The taste is so much better!

Use the coffee press to brew at double strength, making thick, rich coffee. Because of the nature of the process (especially the pressure exerted on the coffee while plunging and the thick, colloidal nature of the resulting brew), this is a satisfying home stand-in for the coffee-bar variety. Ounce for ounce, good double-strength coffee can be substituted for espresso in most any beverage recipe, including those at the end of this chapter.

To steam the *latte,* which means "milk" in Italian, you can use a stovetop or electric steamer designed expressly for this purpose. There are several sturdy stovetop models on the market; one electric plug-in version we recommend is the Salton/Maxim Cappuccino Crazy, which retails for around $50. The greatest advantage of separating brewing and milk steaming mechanisms is that each can achieve the temperature necessary for the best possible result—without sabotaging the other's efforts.

Our industry is fueled by innovation, and new models appear constantly; you may well find a machine at your local store that meets your needs better than the few we've touched upon. Because you have the tools to evaluate the effectiveness of espresso-brewing, you should be able to spot viable new options as they appear. We heartily encourage you to "test-drive" new machines in the company of a knowledgeable retailer, and keep the twin reference points of the commercial machine/grinder ideal in mind, as well as your own expectations and budget.

MANO: THE SKILLED "HAND"

The barista is the highly skilled individual who crafts your espresso beverage. In Italy, the barista is equipped to prepare any kind of drink you can think of, and it is the barista who unites art with the science of espresso.

The barista leaves her signature on your drink in numerous ways. She applies a firm and consistent tamp to the ground coffee. Her keen eyes watch the shots pour, making sure they undulate with the correct speed and form and manifest admirable caramel-like color. It is the barista who steams milk to the perfect froth and temperature and then brings everything together in a prewarmed porcelain demitasse or wide-mouthed cappuccino cup. No matter how advanced or automated, absolutely no machine can do these things on its own.

If you dedicate yourself to learning to make espresso drinks at home, you will have to take on this role. In Italy, the role of the barista is a highly esteemed one and usually a lifelong career. Know that brewing good espresso is not like punching the button on an automatic drip machine. It takes time, energy, and above all, a high level of awareness. Given these things, the ritual of preparing good espresso can become absorbing, fulfilling, and eminently pleasing.

Espresso and Caffeine: *Poco Ma Buono*

The inimitable Italian phrase *poco ma buono* translates as "small but good," which in the case of espresso applies to the small amount of liquid and its relative caffeine content. Despite the strength of its flavor, a shot of espresso contains only about half to two-thirds the caffeine of a 6-ounce cup of drip coffee: approximately 50–70 milligrams, versus 100+ milligrams. Espresso tastes strong because of the pressurized extraction and tiny amount of water forced through the grounds, but the 20-second brew time simply doesn't extract caffeine as thoroughly as water that drips its way through over a period of several minutes. Italians may take the world's briefest coffee breaks, but the modest caffeine content of the espresso they drink allows for many throughout the day.

Basic Espresso Drink Recipes

Espresso: A straight, 1-ounce measure of espresso, also known as a "shot." It is best to brew straight espresso directly into the demitasse in which it will be served so none of its heat or crema is lost. Espresso should be consumed immediately after brewing. Topped with a scant teaspoon of steamed milk foam, it is called an *espresso macchiato* ("marked" or "spotted" in Italian); with a dollop of whipped cream, it is an *espresso con panna* ("with cream"). The first half to three-quarters of the full shot, a *ristretto* or "restricted" shot, can also be served straight or used in beverage recipes. Ristretto shots tend to be sweeter, but not as deep.

Cappuccino: One or more shots of espresso in a glass or porcelain cup, topped with a mixture of half steamed milk and half steamed milk foam. In Italy, this is the traditional morning drink (and is rarely served after noon). A sound proportion to start with is 1 shot in a traditional shallow 6-ounce cup. Increase the amount of milk and foam to dilute; add additional shots to heighten the coffee's "presence."

Caffè Latte: One or more shots of espresso topped with steamed milk, then finished with a 1/4-inch of steamed milk foam. The increased amount of milk further mutes the taste of the espresso (therefore, this is one of the drinks most preferred by beginning espresso drinkers). Try starting with 1 ounce in a 6-ounce cup, add your foam, and taste. Maintain a consistent 5:1 ratio when using larger serveware.

Caffè Mocha: One or more shots of espresso added to a cup holding an ounce of *good* chocolate syrup, then filled with steamed milk (no foam). Most mocha lovers don't call it finished until a garnish of whipped cream is added (whipped cream without sugar or other additives is best). You won't find this delicious espresso milkshake in Italy, but many Americans find it the most appealing of all.

Americano: An American invention, and the ultimate ratio is a matter of personal preference. Dilute one or more shots of espresso with good, fresh, brew-temperature water. You may want to start with 2 shots in a 6-ounce cup, which approximates the proper strength for drip-brewed coffee.

To add flavoring: Start with less; you can always add more. Pour in just enough syrup to cover the bottom of your cup, then continue according to the drink recipe. When flavoring with syrups, always make sure the espresso is mixed in before adding milk to avoid possible curdling of the latter.

To prepare iced espresso beverages: Put ice in the cup first, add your liquid (milk for a latte or water for an iced Americano), and then pour shots of espresso over the top. Mix together. If you want to be extravagant, top it off with a spoonful of steamed milk (somewhat "dry" to prevent melting the uppermost ice). To make an iced mocha, reverse the order: chocolate and espresso first, mixed well. Add milk to fill the cup one-half to three-quarters full. Everything should mix together naturally; if not, help the cause with a spoon. Then add ice, and whipped cream if desired.

Putting Restaurants to the Test

A memorable midafternoon meal in Tuscany, hosted by the beneficent Signor Piero Bambi of the famous La Marzocco espresso machine company, was drawing to a close. It was our first trip to Italy; lunch consisted of five full courses and lasted more than three hours. Thoroughly sated and desperately in need of revival (or a nap), we each turned to order an espresso.

Signor Bambi sliced the air with his hand.

"Do you not know better than that?" he laughed unbelievingly. "Never, *ever* order coffee in a restaurant!"

He went on to pantomime in Chaplinesque style each of the tasks upon which the harried kitchen staff was likely to be focusing, and making our *caffè* was not among them. Signor Bambi's message was clear: In Italy, because you have the choice, order coffee only in a bar where you can watch it being made.

If this advice is necessary in the country where coffee is prepared with greater care than anywhere else in the world, what can one possibly expect here in the United States?

For the Consumer: Insist on Quality

It is sad to say, but a coffee professional's sole motivation for ordering coffee in many restaurants is analytical and diagnostic. Often, the question is not *whether* bad things have been done to the coffee but merely *which ones*. The finer the dining establishment, the more prevalent the problems. Casual, high-volume places are at least forced to brew frequently.

Coffee is usually the last thing customers taste before they settle their bill and gather their coats. It tops off the evening and thus figures significantly in their impression and memory of the overall dining experience. The preparation of this image-fixing beverage, however, is most often delegated to the lowest-paid and lowest-ranked staff members—in other words, the people who have the least time to monitor its quality. Our opinion is that many restaurants are missing a priceless opportunity, and so are their customers.

Why such poor brew from the hands of those who treat other foods with great delicacy and intention? Since the advent of the "bottomless cup" in the 1960s, coffee has been treated like a cheap draw or a necessary condiment rather than as a potentially profitable course deserving of care and investment. Chefs who are so devoted to ingredient quality that they will price an expensive cut of beef or fish perilously close to cost on the menu recoil in horror (and threaten to change brands) when their roaster raises prices by 2¢ a cup. These establishments simply don't consider brewing coffee on par with other forms of cooking. The inattention permitted as a result of the historical switch from vacuum-pot coffee to electric drip has proved the death of good restaurant coffee.

And restaurants are afraid to risk upgrading the quality of their preparation. Ironically, the same cutting-edge places that serve fish still wriggling and refuse orders for steak cooked past medium often justify half-strength cups of coffee as being "the strength our customers want." Emphatically, they continue: "We *can't* have complaints."

If you love coffee and dine out, you are sure to have been frustrated, too. Even in regions where good coffee is widely available in coffee stores, this grim portrait hits close to the truth. Short of sneaking in a personal thermos or to-go cup from the nearest coffee bar—both of which we have seen done—what's a coffee-loving consumer to do?

1. *Scan the menu.* Are flavored coffees listed there? Prices uncharacteristically modest? If so, be warned.

2. *Do a bit of sleuthing.* If brewers are anywhere in evidence, look for a timer close to each pot. Ask about freshness, and never trust anyone who says, with a casual shrug, "Oh, we're always brewing it."

3. *Taste the coffee.* You know what to look for and what's worth the money. If a cup doesn't meet your standards…

4. *Complain.* Do it constructively; restaurants, especially good ones, are responsive to honest, earnestly presented feedback. If no one says anything about the coffee and continues to pay for it, there is no motivation for the

establishment to do any better. If the coffee is truly atrocious, consider sending it back and asking to have it taken off the tab. Wouldn't you do that with a blackened and brittle steak? The management will listen.

Fresh, properly brewed coffee is relatively easy to achieve; you should feel comfortable insisting that every cup be of good quality. A few smart restaurants even offer their discriminating customers fine coffee brewed individually in plunger pots, which is an excellent option.

Espresso demands a far greater level of attention, and when incorporated into restaurant programs it should be accompanied by tremendous care and consistent training. Whatever is offered and regardless of what you order, do us all a favor by insisting that your coffee be good, well-brewed, and fresh.

For the Restaurant: Brewing Standards and Recommendations

While this book is predominantly consumer-focused, we are sure that many of our readers are involved in food service and care about the quality of the coffee they serve. For your benefit, and that of curious consumers, we have included a quick listing of the basic parameters for brewing good restaurant coffee.

DRIP COFFEE

The requirements for good drip coffee in this venue are similar to those for home brewing, but slightly more stringent. The temperature for drip coffee should be

195–205°F, with a total brew cycle of 4–6 minutes. A standard 1/2-gallon pot should be made with a weighed dose (not scooped or otherwise approximated) of 3.5–4.25 dry-weight ounces of freshly roasted and ground coffee.

Below 3.5 ounces and it isn't specialty coffee, no matter how prestigious the label on the beans. Ground coffee needs to be weighed on a scale; the widely available dispensers and combination doser-grinders for drip coffee are extremely inaccurate and cause wild variations in brew strength.

There are significant differences between the quality of drip coffee made on conventional 1/2-gallon pot brewers and that made on the larger pieces of equipment manufactured by American Metal Ware and Fetco. (A nominal capacity for the latter types is 1-1/2 gallons.)

If the coffee is truly freshly roasted and ground just prior to use, the brew basket on a pot brewer will overflow when full amounts of coffee and water are used. Such units were designed before the advent of today's darker, fresher coffee supplies, and getting good results from them requires a bit of improvisation. Coffee for brewing on these units should be either delivered *very* recently preground, or ground and divided into batches by someone on staff the night before they are to be brewed. This allows the coffee to "degas" but still guarantees reasonable freshness. Turning down the spray-over setting on your machine from 64 to 50 or so ounces is another worthwhile trick.

A bit of number crunching will show that brewing into insulated containers is far and away the best choice for most restaurants. Brewed coffee will maintain optimum flavor for about 20 minutes on a burner, and double that or even a little better in an airpot or other well-insulated container not exposed to direct heat.

In addition to possessing superior containers for storing the brewed coffee, the best of the larger shuttle-style brewers come equipped with capacious brew baskets and a water bypass option to prevent overextraction. They boast an electronic thermostat that ensures a better brew temperature and more rapid recovery to brewing temperature between pots. The combined effect of these features, when properly deployed, is the ability to make far better coffee than any smaller brewer is capable of—and the flexibility to focus the cup style to suit the particular coffee(s) being brewed.

The 1-1/2-gallon units are sophisticated adaptations of the classic 3-gallon coffee urn, which because of its favorable coffee-to-paper-filter ratio can also brew magnificent drip coffee. Their only drawback is that the large quantity of finished brew must be sold quickly—within 20 minutes. Sadly, this limitation makes the classic urn the brewer of choice only in very high-volume situations.

ESPRESSO

Espresso should be made to order from coffee ground just prior to brewing. The dose should be 6–7 grams of coffee per shot. A shot measures 1–1.5 fluid ounces (including crema) and has been extracted in 18–24 seconds using water at 192–198°F.

Optimally, a shot intended for drinking straight is pulled directly into a pre-warmed demitasse. All others should be pulled into the containers in which the final beverages will be served, whenever possible.

There are dozens of brands of espresso machines and grinders available. Because of the myriad maintenance and training challenges of operating an espresso bar, it pays to buy from a local, accessible source that can offer you superlative service and support.

If you are planning to run a high-volume operation (300 or more drinks per day), or are an unabashed espresso fanatic, your choices for machines narrow and become more costly in a hurry. In order to guarantee optimum coffee quality regardless of whether the machine is brewing the first shot of the day or serving a line 30 people deep, you need a machine that can balance the heating of the water used for brewing precisely and independently of the high-temperature steam necessary for frothing milk.

With two important exceptions, all commercial espresso machines use a heat exchanger that runs through a single boiler as the source for brewing water. There's nothing wrong with heat exchangers per se—they do a marvelous job of heating water. Unfortunately, they do a less-than-ideal job of balancing the disparate temperature needs of brewing and steaming. This leaves the espresso brewing water subject to undesirable fluctuations in temperature.

The best solution to the problem was invented by the Italian company La Marzocco. Their machine features two independent stainless steel boilers (others use mostly copper) and a precision thermostat capable of controlling brewing water to ± 1°C. La Marzocco's groundbreaking design also provides a unique degree of thermal equilibrium between the water in the dedicated coffee boiler, and the portafilter and other parts of the machine with which the coffee and water come in contact.

The recently introduced Armando espresso machine also features a double boiler. This machine performs similarly to, and is in most key respects a derivative of, the La Marzocco machine.

The net result of the double-boiler machines is a more optimally extracted and quite superior-tasting shot of espresso. The machines possess numerous other functional advantages, and their construction is of substantially higher quality than other units. As you might anticipate, the double-boiler machines are also, on average, twice as expensive as a good heat-exchanger machine.

Many excellent brands of grinder-dosers exist. Once installed, the main issue with these units is maintenance. The grinding burrs need frequent changing (about every 400–500 pounds, depending on the brand).

Many coffee bar operators try to squeeze by with just one grinder, using preground decaf espresso instead of investing in a dedicated machine. The result is often a decaffeinated cup that tastes like stale, strong, instant coffee. Our best advice is to grind all espresso fresh on command and have each piece of your equipment serviced quarterly by a qualified technician.

Customizing Your Coffee

Drinking coffee is about taste and pleasure. Just as having a variety of brewing methods at your disposal can increase enjoyment, so can varying the coffees you drink in accordance with the time of day and season.

There are certainly coffee lovers who see no point in venturing beyond the lush world of the Indonesians, once they discover them. And there are ultra-fastidious tasters for whom all but the most refined washed coffees are mere distractions. There is nothing wrong with sticking close to what you love once you have surveyed the entire range of available flavors, but it is our experience that coffee drinkers greatly increase their enjoyment by trying new things.

The degree of experimentation you seek will of course depend on your own particular tastes, which are themselves fluid—subject to attitude, broader life experience, and your ever-increasing base of coffee knowledge.

Seasonality: Ours and Coffee's

Given sufficient exposure to different coffee varieties, many coffee drinkers find they gravitate toward milder, brighter coffees in the morning and in warm weather. Darker roasts and the earthy richness of Indonesian coffees are often more satisfying later in the day and during darker, chillier seasons.

Another factor that ought to play a larger role in your coffee selection is the seasonality of green coffees themselves. Coffees are usually at their most vibrant during the first six months or so following their arrival at U.S. ports. Beyond this period, they very gradually begin to lose acidity and flavor.

Each country and each region has its own crop cycle. The top Central American coffees are shipped from February through May, meaning that the best of them arrive in late spring and early summer. New-crop Ethiopians start arriving February and continue through June or so. The highest-quality Kenyans begin to trickle in during June and have generally all landed by November.

Indonesian coffees, which are definitely "winter-weight" coffees, are conveniently at their best during that time of year. Peak coffees arrive from November through March or April. With the exception of Papua New Guineas, acidity is not an important attribute of these coffees; "new-" versus "old-" crop issues are therefore much less important.

Artful roasters make subtle modifications to their roasts over time, maximizing what individual coffees have to offer at each stage of their lives. When you consider the fact that most great coffees are available to roasters only once a year, the importance of such customized sculpting through roast becomes particularly obvious.

Flavoring Coffees

Coffee and flavorings have coexisted happily since coffee's very beginning. Some coffee-growing cultures still make a tea from coffee cherries and honey. The Middle Eastern tradition of serving powdered coffee brewed up with cardamom and sugar is only slightly less ancient. In all probability, the tradition of spiking coffee with liqueurs goes back to the wee hours of the night after that first liqueur was invented.

When you begin with a coffee that is itself inherently flavorful, additional flavorings can be used as grace notes that enhance rather than overwhelm. A mid-morning cappuccino topped with a few shards of grated Valrhona chocolate gains appeal without an appreciable increase in calories, while a few drops of fine orange liqueur will do wonders for an after-dinner cup of dark-roasted Guatemala Antigua. What is most important is that you flavor your coffee with ingredients commensurate in quality with the coffees you choose.

THE PERILS OF FLAVORING BY THE BEAN

What the above-mentioned ways of flavoring have in common is that they all involve flavoring coffee by the cup, not by the bean. Coffee that is flavored by the bean—known commercially as "flavored coffee"—has been soaked in chemical flavorings. The advent of this flavoring method is recent and part of the overall explosion of food flavoring that has occurred over the past 25 years.

Those who promote flavored beans draw a tenuous connection between flavored beverages and flavored beans, but neither the raw ingredients nor the results have much in common. Such roasters also try to represent flavored beans as a "bridge" to finer coffees, but this is rather like hoping consumers of wine coolers will one day come to discussing the finer points of vintage Bordeaux. Extensive retail experience shows us that it just doesn't happen.

Flavored coffees are created by dousing beans of no great pedigree in concentrated liquid flavorings, often then adding botanicals such as cocoa powder, orange peel, or nuts. The flavorings are typically mixtures of natural and artificial substances held together with some kind of spreading agent, usually the solvent propylene glycol. This is designed to give the coffees a long shelflife; such treatment enables the flavorings to remain potent during the weeks and months the beans will sit in bins prior to purchase and consumption.

Many find that the aromas of these flavorings have appeal. Unfortunately, there is little harmony between aroma and actual flavor—and certainly not what one can achieve by individually flavoring a pot or cup of coffee. More problematic in the retail context is the problem of contamination; flavored beans scent every fixture and grinder they touch, more often than not permanently.

Like workers in a perfumery, individuals who spend regular hours in a store or other environment permeated with the smell of flavorings gradually lose their sensitivity. They lose sight (or, rather smell) of the extent to which these flavorings have taken over. And take over they do: Unless they are sealed in an airtight container, flavored coffees will communicate their aromas to any other neighboring straight (i.e., nonflavored) or other flavored coffee that is left similarly unsealed. Over the last 10 years, in hundreds of cuppings performed on purportedly straight coffees purchased from retailers across the country, more than half of all samples were indelibly tainted with second-hand flavorings.

In some parts of the country, flavored coffees have virtually no presence in the marketplace. In others, they account for 50 percent or more of total sales. Some retailers carry "flavoreds" because they love them; many more do so reluctantly, in response to consumer demand. The most serious, product-driven stores won't carry flavoreds at all. These stores are remarkable for the courage of their convictions and for the fact that they smell like coffee, *pure coffee,* when you walk in the door.

THE JOYS OF FLAVORING BY THE CUP

As a culture, Americans are possessed of a remarkable sweet tooth. If you hunger for additional flavoring in your coffee, we recommend trying one or more of the following.

Syrups

One of the best ways to sate the preference for sweet without sacrificing essential coffee flavor is to add flavored, simple-sugar syrups to each individual cup or pot of coffee. These syrups were originally developed, ironically, to impart coffee flavors to Italian ices. Made and sold by companies such as Torani, Monin, and DaVinci, they constitute a rising trend in espresso bars. Most manufacturers also provide a small bottles that are ideal for use at home.

Natural flavors such as hazelnut, vanilla, and almond are typically the most harmonious complements to coffee. Look for those with a higher proportion of extract relative to sugar content. To flavor your cup, add just enough to cover the bottom of the cup. Pour in the coffee, then adjust the amount of flavoring to your own taste. We recommend this approach because it is always easier to increase the amount of flavoring you use than to dilute an over-doctored cup.

Note: When using syrups, add coffee before mixing in anything else. Syrups have a tendency to curdle dairy products, but won't if coffee is already in the game.

Spices

Your own taste buds should be your guide, but here are a few of the classics:

Cinnamon: Because adding ground cinnamon directly to a cup of coffee creates a bitter aftertaste, try placing one whole cinnamon stick in each cup you serve. The resulting aroma is spicy and satisfying.

Cardamom: A couple of cardamom pods tossed into a fresh pot or cup of brewed coffee give forth a tantalizing aroma.

Chocolate: Feathered across the top of a caffè latte, fresh shavings of a fine dark chocolate, such as Valrhona, are sublime. To complement other coffee beverages, just keep small chunks handy for melting and nibbling.

Alcohol/Liqueur

Use the same measurement as you would with flavoring syrups—just enough to cover the bottom of the cup—and get experimental with your pet liquors. There are no hard and fast rules here. Traditional favorites include Sambuca, Frangelico, Grand Marnier, and Creme de Cacao.

Coffee and Food

In virtually every book on beverages, you will find a section like this. And while there is certainly no shortage of recommended pairings for fine wine or good beer, such is not the case with coffee.

Frankly, Americans are notorious for serving weak coffee as an accompaniment to meals. However, Europeans and other historically dedicated consumers of high-quality beans know that coffee is an assertively flavored drink that is best appreciated alone or in the company of a limited range of foodstuffs.

Coffee with breakfast is the most natural coupling, providing warmth, stimulation, and a richly aromatic and flavorful contrast to foods that are typically mild in nature. During the day, coffee is at its best savored solo. After dinner, the beverage provides palate-cleansing contrast to rich desserts, especially those containing chocolate—which at *its* best offers a combination of bitterness and darkly fruity vinosity that is a close kin to coffee.

C H A P T E R   I I

Issues in the Marketplace

For centuries, coffeehouses have been gathering places for the discussion and debate of every imaginable spiritual and temporal issue. Coffee and controversy just plain go together. Combine this history of provocation with a trade focused on brewing exotic liquids to entirely subjective standards, berries produced almost exclusively in Third World nations, and a bastion of industry leaders who themselves came of age in the tempestuous 1960s—and you have a mighty heady brew!

In this chapter, we will touch on some of the hottest issues in today's specialty coffee marketplace: decaffeination methods and caffeine, organic coffees, and coffee pricing. None of these discussions is meant to serve as the last word on its topic. Specialty coffee is a very young industry and continues to evolve rapidly. The consumers who care about quality and are willing to fund it through their purchasing habits are helping to bring about some exciting changes, ranging from improved wages on coffee farms to better-tasting decaf. If you are one of these proactive coffee lovers, we hope that the information and opinions presented in this chapter will help you keep quality—at all levels—coming your way.

Decaffeination and Caffeine

No beverage has been the target of more scientific scrutiny than coffee, and for obvious reasons. First and foremost, nearly every adult drinks it. In coffee, we have a beverage of negligible caloric value that is consumed by vast numbers of people for its pleasurable flavor and stimulating effects.

From a health standpoint, it would be enormously convenient if such a beverage by itself were the cause of any major affliction; one would only need to get rid of the coffee in order to eliminate the affliction. Yet despite intense investigation, the evidence to date shows that moderate consumption poses few problems for the majority of adults.

WHAT IS CAFFEINE?

Caffeine ($C_8H_{10}N_4O_2$) is a compound found naturally in coffee and more than 60 other plants. It's an odorless, slightly bitter-tasting solid that dissolves easily in water or alcohol. Beverages containing caffeine have been used medicinally for centuries; today, it is still an important ingredient in many over-the-counter analgesics. If you have ever sipped coffee, tea, or a caffeinated soft drink, you are probably well-acquainted with its stimulating effects.

There is some debate about how caffeine actually works, but the most contemporary theories hold that caffeine doesn't hype us up so much as it prevents us from slowing down. Caffeine attaches to the neural receptors that normally attract adenosine, a chemical that is produced in the body and which exerts a calming effect on the activity of the brain. When caffeine, and not adenosine, is lodged at the ends of these receptors, the firing of cells increases—and we experience a corresponding increase in mental stimulation. Note that this is an increase in speed, not smarts; caffeine makes your brain work faster, but it doesn't add to the raw material you already have.

The "caffeine headache" many associate with a sudden curtailing of coffee or soft drink consumption is caused by the reverse phenomenon. The routine presence of caffeine motivates the body to manufacture additional adenosine receptors; the body knows when the chemical isn't bonding in the volume it should and so works to create more opportunity. When caffeine is withdrawn, therefore, there is an abundance of receptor sites for adenosine to fill. The physiological reaction is a dilation of blood vessels in the brain—ouch! Fortunately, this reaction is short-lived; most people report their headaches subside between one and two days after the initial change in consumption habits.

One key to embracing moderation with coffee, as with most foods, is finding good flavor. A modest pint of Guinness stout has a far greater flavor impact than much larger quantities of the pale pilsner-type American beer. And, because of the stout's increased flavor, great satisfaction can be had from moderate amounts. The same holds true for a cup of well-made, full-strength fine coffee. Many coffee lovers have discovered that a few truly flavorful cups meet their needs better than a parade of mainstream mega-mugs. Indeed, it appears likely that the availability of excellent brewed coffee is one of the primary reasons that the consumption of decaffeinated coffee is slowly waning.

This is not to say that decaf is outmoded. Both caffeine-sensitive consumers and regular coffee drinkers who want a less stimulating after-dinner cup continue their search for decaf with flavor. In fact, market research tells us that most decaf is consumed by "dual drinkers"—people who drink both decaf and regular—and that when making coffee purchases they prioritize taste above all else.

DECAF COFFEE:
PREMIUM PRODUCT WITHOUT A PREMIUM PRICE?

Truth be told, the consumers who drink decaf bear partial responsibility for the fact that much of it tastes fairly wretched. Here is why.

Decaffeination plants are enormously expensive facilities to build, and the processes used are sophisticated, costly, and time-consuming. More important, to end up with decent decaf you have to start with superlative green coffee beans. Every decaffeination process strips a great deal of flavor from the coffee; if you want a product with any kind of flavor post-decaffeination, you have to invest in the highest-quality—and therefore most expensive—beans.

Premium beans plus a costly process: It is only logical to assume that decaf drinkers would pay extra for the added value. Yet in the majority of cases, they don't. In a retail setting, consumers will pay more for whole-bean decaf, but not much more. And most consumers would be outraged if a coffee bar or restaurant charged 30 percent more for a cup of decaf than for regular coffee. This reticence has an obvious and negative effect on the quality of coffees offered in decaffeinated form. If customers won't pay more, the only economically viable solution for the roaster is to start out with less expensive, lower-quality coffee—and *this* yields the poor taste decaf drinkers complain about.

THE DECAFFEINATION PROCESS

The first step in every decaffeination method is to open the pores of green coffee beans by plumping them up in hot water. This makes the caffeine, which is spread throughout the bean, more accessible. No matter how this is done, it's not a gentle process.

The next stage involves using a solvent to remove the caffeine. In what is commonly called the "traditional," or "direct contact," method, that solvent will be either methylene chloride or ethyl acetate. Both of these chemicals are common, and very selective in what they remove from the bean.

In the Swiss Water® process, activated charcoal is used to draw caffeine from a caffeine-and-water solution which itself has been extracted from the beans. More exotic still, "supercritical" CO_2, or carbon dioxide under extremely high pressure, may be used. The latter method, while it shows great promise, is not in wide use for specialty coffee. (The only supercritical plant in the United States is currently used exclusively for mass-market products sold as "naturally decaffeinated.")

How much caffeine is actually taken out? In order to be sold as decaf, at least 97 percent of the original caffeine must be removed. In practice, this number is usually closer to 99 percent. That means 99 percent of the caffeine by weight contained in arabica coffee, which is already half of what's in robusta coffee. Decaffeinated specialty coffee clocks in at a low milligram or two per cup versus over a hundred milligrams for a cup of the leaded stuff.

After the caffeine is removed, the beans are carefully rinsed and dried. Sadly, no matter what the method, the result of decaffeination is significant loss of flavor and aroma. This doesn't mean that decaf technology isn't sophisticated—it is just another indicator of the fact that coffee is incredibly delicate and complex. And it also leads one again to the conclusion that if the goal is great-tasting decaf, the most flavorful beans—which are, of course, also the most costly—should be selected for processing.

THE CHEMICAL CONTROVERSY: FACT VS. FALLACY

Consumer concern regarding chemical residue as a result of the decaffeination process has fueled the demand for chemical-free decaf, but to date these fears seem more phobic than well-founded. The FDA allows solvent to be present in the amount of 10 parts per million. Residual levels of methylene chloride in just-decaffeinated green coffees amount to a few parts per million. There is no evidence that any solvent survives the combined heat of the roasting and brewing processes. You may remember that coffee is roasted at over 400°F; methylene chloride has a boiling point of about 114°F.

IN SEARCH OF FULLER FLAVOR

The amount of flavor lost during decaffeination varies with the coffee and the process. As you might expect, coffees with intense character survive the best: Sumatra and Kenya are perennial performers. Coffees that are decaffeinated using methylene chloride retain the most flavor, followed by the less commonly available ethyl acetate decafs.

Both of these processes are likely to either go unlabelled at the retail level, or to be sold with a convenient catch-all term: "European processed," "traditional process," or "direct contact." This is not to say that every traditionally decaffeinated coffee will be superior to those processed by other methods. In order to take full advantage of the more selective nature of these solvents, roasters must personally select top-quality coffees for decaffeination (a practice known as "toll" decaffeination) and enlist the services of a superior processor such as Germany's Coffein Company. Such customized processing increases both cost and quality dramatically over normal "off-the-rack" offerings.

In recent years, The Swiss Water process has been improved considerably, and the quality of coffees generally selected for decaffeination with this method is quite good. But because water is chemically less selective as a solvent, considerably more flavor is "washed out" of the coffee when this process is used. The resulting coffee is decent-tasting, but has very little specific varietal flavor. That said, we must point out that for many consumers, the appeal of Swiss Water has less to do with flavor than with the desire to support a chemical-free decaffeination process. Because a coffee has been Swiss Water-processed does not mean the coffee itself is chemical-free—that is a matter related to organic agricultural practices, and an entirely different issue. What buying Swiss Water decaf does mean is that you are supporting a decaffeination process free of chemicals and the possible contamination of both coffee and environment.

Supercritical CO_2 decafs, should they ever become widely available, may provide decaf lovers with methylene chloride-level flavor and Swiss Water-like peace of mind. Kraft General Foods owns both the Swiss Water facility and North America's supercritical CO_2 plant, so there is some hope that top-quality supercritical CO_2 decafs will become more prevalent as interest in fine coffee continues to grow.

HOW TO GET GOOD DECAF

Lost for good, no matter what the decaffeination process, are aromatic subtlety and all but a little acidity. If you love these qualities in coffee, sip a small cup of the real thing early in the day—there's no alternative. Fortunately, when you want a heartier and heavier-bodied cup of decaf, these flavors are easier to find.

Search out a roaster who cares enough about good-tasting decaf to offer top-quality coffee decaffeinated using methylene chloride or ethyl acetate. Look for African or Indonesian single-origin coffees, or blends containing high percentages of either. If you like dark roast flavor, you will be the happiest of all decaf drinkers; this is one coffee flavor that can be achieved as easily with decaf as it can with regular caffeinated coffees, regardless of the processing method that is used.

Be warned: Because of the color changes that occur during processing, any properly roasted decaf will look dangerously dark. Don't be fooled by the foreboding color; it is not an accurate indicator of depth of roast.

Because a number of flavor oils are removed during decaffeination, you need to do something to bring the flavor back up to par. Use at least 20 percent more coffee than usual, or switch to a brewing method—such as a coffee press or espresso machine—that amps up the coffee's body.

Organic Coffees

Organic coffee is frequently presented to consumers as a product whose purchase will right many wrongs, all at the same time. Promoters have a tendency to package complicated social, political, and agricultural issues together and then, all too often, reduce their complexity to misleading sound bites. As much as we sometimes wish it were possible, these issues contain too many shades of gray for accurate reproportioning to bumper-sticker size.

Coffees that have been certified to be organically grown make up 1 to 2 percent of the total specialty coffee sales, and this percentage continues to increase steadily. These coffees are seen by many consumers as simply an extension of the local, organically grown produce sold in natural foods stores (and increasingly in mainstream supermarkets as well). On the surface, this translation from local produce to coffee beans seems logical; coffee and lettuce are both agricultural products. In reality, however, the differences outweigh the similarities.

More than One Kind of Farming

These differences begin with the fact that there is no such thing as "local" coffee—unless you live in Hawaii. Coffee is produced almost exclusively in developing nations, whose priorities, growing conditions, and broader concerns differ greatly from our own. A relationship with coffee allows us to travel vicariously through intriguing parts of the developing world; accompanying the excitement of this kind of exploration is a responsibility to try and see coffee through the eyes of the people who grow it.

There are somewhere in the neighborhood of 80 coffee-producing countries, and thousands of farmers within each one. Accurate generalizations about horticultural practices and other aspects of coffee growing are therefore quite difficult to make.

In fact, perhaps the only generalization we can offer with assurance is that growing coffee is not an endeavor to be undertaken lightly. As much as farmers in the United States feel they routinely operate close to the margin of survival, this feeling takes on a whole new meaning in the context of the Third World.

Five entire years must pass between the time a young coffee seedling is planted and the time its first full crop is ready, and the average productive life span of a tree is around 15 years. With a total yield of about one pound of coffee a year per tree, a modest-sized farm has to cultivate over a million individually nurtured seedlings in its nursery each year to survive. In addition, at the higher elevations where good coffees grow, many other agricultural crops won't. Coffee is not something a farmer gets into—or out of—easily.

Commercial Coffee

Visit a lowland coffee farm in Brazil, whose crop will end up in cans at the local supermarket. Most likely, you will see farming that looks very much like everyday, large-scale North American agribusiness. As much work as possible is relegated to machinery, and human workers don't seem particularly invested in their tasks. Fungicides, fertilizers, and pesticides sourced from large American manufacturers are everywhere in evidence. Everything you see is indicative of the farm's focus: big crop size, high yield, and little else.

Traditional Plantations

Top-quality specialty coffees are grown under totally different conditions. They are situated high in the mountains, at altitudes that usually range from 4,000 to over 6,000 feet. Daytime temperatures land in the 70s, humidity is moderate, and the nights are positively chilly. These conditions and the rocky, volcanic soil typical of these areas greatly reduce outbreaks of the insect and fungus infestations that plague lowland tropical crops.

When you visit a hundred-year-old farm in Guatemala, Costa Rica, or Nicaragua, you are likely to encounter a farmer who is anything but ignorant regarding the health of his land, his coffee, or the people associated with both. Chances are excellent that one of the farm's owners holds a degree in agriculture from a U.S. college.

Soil is tested regularly, and the leaves of protective shade trees provide compost for the coffee plants they shelter. Large plantings of fruit, corn, black beans, and other food stuffs sustain the farm and its workers, and provide colorful contrast to the well-tended coffee trees. Vigorous, tropical weeds are controlled with machetes, not herbicides, despite the fact that such labor-intensive weed control costs several times more. There is no question that this approach is chosen because it's better for the land and workers in the long run.

Coffees grown in this manner are the backbone of the specialty coffee trade. They have proven their sustainability in a way that is profoundly important for any farm, and especially so for one in a so-called developing nation: The crop they produce fetches a high price, year in and year out, because of its superior quality. When you visit such farms, the pride in quality is evident at every level—not the least in the treatment of the workers tending them, who typically enjoy wages, benefits, and working conditions that are among the best in their countries.

These traditional farms may be environmentally aware, but they are not organic. Nitrogen-based fertilizer is applied, and while the use of systemic pesticides is rare, spot application of pesticides and fungicides in the event of an infestation is not uncommon. The crop is precious; no one wants to see it ruined.

Coffee cherries, along with other farm waste, are composted and used, but unlike the garbage-rich United States, these Central American highlands don't produce large amounts of organic waste suitable for compost. Without fertilizer, coffee plants become much more susceptible to disease, while yields can decrease by 50 percent or more. Farmers in such prestigious areas understandably question whether planting twice the acreage for an equivalent yield is really more ecologically responsible, and whether consumers would pay double or triple current prices for already costly coffee.

"Backyard" Organics

In many parts of Africa and Arabia, coffee is grown entirely without the use of chemical fertilizers, herbicides, or pesticides. Particularly in Ethiopia, substantial amounts of coffee are still harvested from wild native trees. It is not that farmers consciously refrain from using such aids, but rather that the aids are simply unavailable—and would be prohibitively expensive even if they were accessible.

In Indonesia, coffee is grown mostly as a cash crop alongside other similarly purposed crops on small family farms, usually less than three acres in size. These coffees, too, are grown primarily organically. As with the Africans, however, they lack third-party certification and thus cannot be sold as organic coffee in the marketplace. Such certification is extremely expensive, and many farmers regard the idea of paying a foreigner a fortune to fly in and bestow a blessing on the normal way of doing things as borderline certifiable!

Certified Organics
The existence of coffees that are certified to be organically grown is a relatively recent phenomenon. The certification process, which is implemented by a number of independent agencies including the OCIA (Organic Crop Improvement Association), the OGBA (Organic Growing and Buying Association), and Europe-based Demeter, is complex. Each certifying organization's requirements are different, but generally involve initial visits to farms, intensive farmer education in composting and natural methods of pest control and prevention, transitional periods where necessary, and regular inspections of the farm by the certifying agency.

Most farms that produce certified organic coffees are located in Peru and Mexico. These countries are relatively easy to access from the United States, and possess plenty of farmers willing to try new approaches that might bring higher prices for their coffee. In a handful of cases, these farms produce coffee that is both excellent in quality and residue-free, but for the most part they are "projects" instigated by foreigners who are focusing on their own social and environmental agendas.

The end result is that such ideologically motivated coffee projects are started in areas that aren't ideally suited for the growing of good coffee. Pests may be a greater problem than elsewhere because of this; fighting them and nourishing the coffee demands more resources than it should. Typically, neither the farmers nor their sponsors have substantial experience with coffee or coffee growing. Most problematic of all is the fact that the market premiums paid for the coffee are unreliable because they are based solely on organicity instead of quality.

This arrangement is of dubious long-term value, because consumers will never get from these farms the superior flavor they expect from organic products. These coffee projects, though they are motivated by the desire to provide aid, bring new coffee farmers into an industry for which they have none of the tools necessary to succeed.

To their benefit, more and more farmers are recognizing the importance of quality in achieving consistent premiums. There are currently a handful of organic farms—situated in choice microclimates in Mexico, Guatemala, Costa Rica, and Indonesia—that produce world-class organic coffees.

HEALTH CONCERNS

Regardless of what sort of coffee you buy, there is little reason to be concerned about pesticide or other residue ending up in your cup. Very little of what is applied can make it through the coffee's protective layers (cherry skin, pulp, parchment, and silverskin) to reach the bean. And all beans are processed extensively, then roasted at exceedingly high temperatures, before appearing in a bag or bin.

In this sense, coffee is far removed from other types of produce that you consume essentially "as is" right out of the soil or off the tree. The more persuasive reasons to buy organic coffees, in our opinion, have to do with which sort of agriculture you wish to support. We believe that anyone who invests in the earth and their fellow humans enough to nurture the conditions that yield top-quality coffee is eminently deserving of such support, and those who grow top-quality organic coffees—whether or not the coffees are certified—are especially so.

A RELATED ISSUE: TREATMENT OF WORKERS

Not being experts on the subject of worker's rights or child labor laws, we can not speak exhaustively on these matters. On behalf of experts in the specialty coffee industry, however, we can say with significant authority that the general outcry against minimum wage in Guatemala and other "unfair" practices is somewhat misguided.

Michael C. Glenister, a specialty green-coffee importer with Amcafé, Inc., is a primary member of the International Relations Committee of the Specialty Coffee Association of America (SCAA). It is his responsibility to research conditions and issues at origin—in the different countries where coffee is grown—and bring information back to the coffee-consuming public. Here are his views:

My personal experience with all the estate owners and managers I know and buy coffee from—from very large to very small operations, from Brazil to Zimbabwe—is that they are, as a group, very socially conscious. They feel a deep responsibility to their staff and their countries.

Estates employ large permanent staffs, and almost without exception provide staff members with company housing for their families, usually with free medical care and schooling. These jobs are highly sought after by the local population. Because of spiraling population growth and the rising unemployment of most coffee producing countries, they represent a "passport" to a secure income with benefits—often much better positions than can be found in other industries or government employment.

It is very important that our retail customers understand that in all coffee producing countries there are strict labor laws. In all the cases I personally know of, estate owners and managers not only abide by these laws, but far exceed local minimum salary and benefit levels.[1]

As a parallel to the organic issue, it would not be illogical to assume, particularly in Central America, that the tragic civil rights violations to which people have been subjected might be replicated on coffee farms (usually called *fincas*). It has been our experience, however, and the experience of virtually every other long-time professional in this field, that this is not the case.

Because coffee is a long-time endeavor, growers depend on the expertise and dedication of their employees. Unlike executives in many United States businesses, successful farmers know the quality of their crop is directly proportional to their treatment of their workers. Coffee fincas are often rural outposts that provide substantial benefits packages to their employees: housing, schools,

[1] ©1995 by Michael C. Glenister, used with permission. First published in the Specialty Coffee Association of America newsletter, *In Good Taste,* in April 1995.

medical facilities, extra land for growing food crops. The growers know they must take good care of their workers, including the seasonal pickers, to keep them coming back to harvest each year.

When concerned individuals here take issue with finca wages, we urge them to look beyond the American dollar equivalent and consider the relative cost—and quality—of living. Thus translated, the daily wage for working on a coffee farm often far outstrips the North American pay and benefits awarded for even more prestigious work.

In addition, many roasters work with aid organizations that help growers build schools and hospitals, provide off-season work alternatives, and provide other resources for their employees. One very active organization that focuses its efforts directly on the people of coffee-growing areas is Coffee Kids, headquartered in Providence, Rhode Island (see Appendix B).

So where do you buy coffee that expresses your convictions? We wish we could give you a simple answer. Develop a clear understanding of what your dollars, paid to different venues, will end up supporting. Decide precisely what it is that you are willing, or not willing, to support.

Many of the great foodstuffs we love are threatened by hybridization, mechanization, and automation, and the welfare of both people and planet are at risk as a result of these practices. Where coffee is concerned, we believe in diverting specialty dollars toward those farms that grow old species, treat their people well, and realize that quality is something that involves people, the planet, and the way we all interact. These coffees are offered by roasters who are knowledgeable, nurture long-term relationships with their growers, and are committed to sustainable quality.

The Price of "C"

For the most part, the internal mechanics of green-coffee pricing remain the concern of exporters, importers, market speculators, and roasters. In the mid 1990s, however, because of a series of devastating frosts followed by drought in Brazil, coffee lovers saw retail and restaurant prices rise with unprecedented haste. The suddenness of these increases sparked a reasonable amount of alarm among the coffee-loving public, and rumors of shortages propelled many coffee drinkers to pursue a better understanding of the relationship between the commodity coffee market and the cost per specialty cup.

THE "C" CONTRACT MARKET

There are two major coffee markets in the world. One, in London, concerns itself exclusively with the buying and selling of robusta coffee. The "C" contract market of the Coffee, Sugar & Cocoa Exchange located in New York City's World Trade Center handles the trade of arabica coffee. When considering pricing for specialty coffee, therefore, the "C" market becomes the focus of attention.

Originally a tool for risk management, the "C" market currently serves three functions: it is a playground for speculators, acts as an indicator of the baseline cost for low-grade arabica beans, and provides a floating starting point from which specialty coffees are priced.

The coffee market is what is called a "futures" market. The rise and fall of prices are indicative of what market traders expect to happen down the road; pricing rarely corresponds with the actual or current balance of supply and demand. In addition, the speculators playing the market tend to make it less stable and inflate—or deflate— regular price movements. These speculators aren't all bad; their activity provides necessary cash flow to the market. Speculators move vast amounts of money in and out of every traded commodity, from soybeans to pork bellies.

For every contract traded on the "C" market, 37,500 pounds of arabica coffee are bought, sold, or transferred. Contracts are priced by the pound in U.S. dollars. A market increase of one penny means each contract automatically shifts up in value by $375.

The "C" indicator price, however, does not correspond to a specific, actual coffee; it is a basis against which real coffees are sold. Lower-grade coffee destined for the mass market sells at prices that may range from well under "C" (a "discount") to several cents above it (a "differential"). Specialty coffees, meanwhile, are sold in two ways: at a substantial premium differential on top of the "C" price, or on an outright, take-it-or-leave-it basis. An average Colombian Supremo, for example, might be priced at "C" +32¢, meaning 32 cents above the month's "C," while a Kona Extra Fancy might be offered for a flat $6.60 per pound. When "C" is low, the differential for a fine specialty coffee typically adds another 50% to the total price tag.

Because the "C" market is a futures market, all who participate in it take risks. Specialty roasters operate with additional constraints. Because top quality beans are rare, they can't make purchases too far in advance but instead are forced to buy coffees strictly on the basis of actual lot samples. Market fluctuations have an especially devastating effect on growers who strive to produce the highest quality beans; many are moving toward outright pricing in order to step away from a vehicle that no longer serves their interests. Proponents of fair trade and sustainable agriculture have long advocated instituting a floor price of $1.20 per pound, which would place farmers less at the mercy of speculators and allow them to count on breaking even. Producing truly fine coffee takes a great deal of extra effort. It is appropriate that we, as consumers, be willing to pay for that.

WHEN BRAZIL SNEEZES

After a long coffee buyer's hiatus, during which the world market was flush with coffee and prices remained artificially low, a convergence of forces caused coffee prices to skyrocket in the spring and summer of 1994. For the first time in many years, coffee drinkers were confronted with direct and sudden price increases almost everywhere.

Because of six straight years of low prices, coffee had turned into a losing proposition for many. Farms were abandoned, trees went untended. In the absence of proper pruning, fertilization, and so on, yields declined and pests became a large problem. The continually growing interest in higher-quality specialty coffees continued to fuel worldwide competition for the best grades.

Finally, destructive frosts in Brazil damaged both trees and beans, further tightening the world's supply. Brazil is the world's largest coffee producer, and an old coffee trade cliché maintains, "When Brazil sneezes, the rest of the world catches a cold."

As we discussed in Chapter 5, "Regional Character," Brazilian coffees take up very little space in most specialty roasters' warehouses. But a shortfall in the Brazilian crop places immediate pressure on every other coffee crop, resulting in 1994 in an unprecedented 300 percent increase in the "C" indicator price over the space of three months.

Interestingly enough, when competition for good coffee stiffens, the first buyers to abandon ship and buy lower grades are usually the large U.S. roasters. Europe and Japan have been far more dedicated to quality in their purchasing, often underwriting growing activities in specific origin countries in exchange for first choice of the exports. They act on a thorough understanding of the life cycle of coffee.

Of course, it doesn't hurt their cause that coffee prices worldwide are based on U.S. dollars. Even steep differentials look like Monopoly money to buyers thinking in yen or Deutschmarks. This country's specialty roasters, however, feel the impact of every penny. Thus when prices on the world market rise, you almost certainly find that the consistently superior coffees are offered by roasters willing to pay top dollar.

GREAT VALUE REGARDLESS OF PRICE

Rising prices inevitably inspire a certain amount of fear. When one sits down to consider the numbers, however, specialty coffee always comes up as a great value. One pound of fine coffee—about 4,000 hand-picked beans—yields 40 fabulous cups of full-strength coffee. At $10 per pound, that is still only 25 cents per cup when you make your coffee at home. Paying similar prices for wine, you'd be securing a fabulous bottle for about $1.50.

APPENDIX A

Glossary of Tasting Terms

Paraphrased with permission from the Allegro Coffee Company
Coffee Specialist's Manual, ©*1994 by Allegro Coffee Company.*

Aftertaste—The sensation of brewed coffee vapors, ranging
from carbony to chocolatey, spicy to turpeny, as they are
released from the residue remaining in the mouth after
swallowing.

Alkaline—A dry, clawing sensation at the back of the
tongue caused by alkaline and phenolic compounds that
have bitter but not necessarily displeasing tastes;
characteristic of dark roasts and some Indonesian
coffees.

Aroma—The odor or fragrance of brewed coffee. *Bouquet* is
a less frequently used term, often employed to refer to
the smell of coffee grounds. Aroma is often distinctive
and complex; terms used to describe it include
caramelly (candy- or syrup-like), carbony (for dark
roasts), chocolatey, fruity, floral, malty (cereal-like),
rich, round, and spicy.

Astringent—A puckering, salty sensation felt on the anterior
sides of the tongue when coffee is first sipped.

Baked—A taste and odor taint that gives coffee a flat bouquet and insipid taste. This taint is caused by the application of too little heat over too long a period during roasting (specifically, when roasts take longer than approximately 18 minutes).

Bitter—A basic taste sensation perceived primarily at the back of the tongue. Dark roasts are intentionally bitter; otherwise, bitterness is primarily associated with overextraction.

Bland—The pale, insipid flavor often found in low-grown coffees. Underextracted coffee is also bland.

Briny—A salty sensation caused by exposure to excessive heat after the brewing is complete.

Buttery—Rich and oily in flavor and texture, characteristic of some Indonesian varietals (for example, Sulawesi).

Caramelized—A sweet, almost-burnt, syrupy flavor not unlike the experience of caramelized sugar.

Clean—The opposite of dirty, and a characteristic of all fine washed coffees.

Earthy—A positive characteristic when applied to dry processing; the herbal, musty, mushroom-like range of flavors characteristic of Indonesian varietals. For washed coffees, tasting "earthy" is a defect.

Exotic—Characteristic of the coffees from East Africa, exotic refers to unusual flavor notes such as floral and berry-like (containing black currant or blueberry notes, for example). Conversely, Latin American coffees, whose characteristic clean, acidy flavors provide the standard of reference, are generally not exotic.

Ferment—A taste fault in the coffee beans that produces a highly objectionable spoiled-fruit taste. Ferment is the result of enzymatic activity that occurs during the drying process, changing sugars to acids in the green coffee beans. Unlike dirtiness and mustiness, which can be disguised by dark roasting, ferment becomes worse the longer it cooks. It is the most dreaded and common defect found in washed coffees, and tasters spend a lot of time looking for it. As a result, they often have a hard time bringing themselves to drink coffees that possess the berry-like wildness of naturally processed Ethiopian varieties. Ferment is of this same character, but carried to an extreme.

Flat—An odor taint that occurs as a result of aromatic compounds departing from beans during the staling process in both whole-bean and ground coffee, or during the holding process in brewed coffee.

Fruit-like—A descriptor that refers to the natural aroma of berries, and that also correlates with the perception of high acidity. It should be distinguished from fruity, which is the first stage of the taste defect ferment.

Grassy—A taste and odor defect that gives coffee the character of newly mown alfalfa or green grass.

Green—An herbal, grassy character caused by incomplete development of flavor due to improper roasting. It may also be present in the early pickings of a new harvest.

Hard—A harsh, medicinal, iodine-like flavor defect often caused by letting cherries dry on the tree. It is found primarily in lower grades of Brazilian coffee.

Insipid—The lifeless flavor of coffee brewed from stale beans.

Mellow—A term used to describe a well-balanced coffee of low to medium acidity.

Mild—Denotes a coffee with harmonious, delicate flavors. For example, fine, high-grown Central American coffees are often described as mild. Mild is also a coffee trade term for arabica coffee grown anywhere in the world outside of Brazil.

Musty—An odor taint giving coffee beans a moldy odor. This taint is caused by the presence of fungus on or in beans during drying or shipment.

Neutral—This quality is characterized by the absence of any predominant taste sensation on any part of the tongue when a coffee is first sipped.

Nutty—A descriptor that refers to the aroma of fresh nutmeats, usually accompanied by specifics such as walnut-like.

Past-crop—A distinct woody flavor, accompanied by loss of acidity and found in green coffees held in storage for more than a year.

Quakery—A taste taint that gives brewed coffee a pronounced peanutty flavor. This taint is caused by including unripe, green coffee cherries in the harvest;

after roasting, the beans remain light in color and markedly undeveloped.

Rubbery—An intense, burnt-rubber character usually found in robusta coffees and caused by allowing the coffee fruit to begin drying on the shrub.

Scorched—A visual and taste defect that is a more severe relative of tipping (burning the ends of beans by applying excessive heat during roasting). The flat surfaces of scorched beans appear and are charred; coffee brewed from these beans leaves an unpleasant, smoky-burnt aftertaste.

Soft—Is a tasting term used for low-acid coffees such as the Indonesians. Soft coffees may also be described as mellow or sweet.

Sour—A primary taste perceived mainly on the posterior sides of the tongue. This taste is characteristic of light-roasted coffees.

Spicy—An aroma or flavor that recalls a particular spice: peppery, cardamom-like, cedar cigar box–like.

Strong—A general descriptor that refers to a large presence of flavor and aroma, or to the relative proportion of soluble solids to water in a given brew.

Sweet—A general term that refers to coffees which are smooth and palatable.

Tangy—An aggressive sourness almost fruit-like in nature; related to winyness. Fine, high-grown Costa Rican coffees are frequently described as being tangy.

Thin—Lacking in flavor and watery in body; characteristic of low-grown coffees.

Wild—A descriptor that indicates extreme flavor characteristics. It can be a defect, or a positive attribute. Wild denotes odd, racy, even gamy nuances of flavor and aroma. Ethiopian coffees, especially Harrar and Djimmah, are the textbook examples.

Winy—Despite all the jokes about "whiny" coffees, winy is a desirable flavor quality that implies characteristics of the finest red wines. Kenya coffees are classic examples: heady and intoxicating!

Woody—A taste characteristic primarily of past-crop coffees. This flavor, when less severe, may also be referred to as strawy.

APPENDIX B

Equipment Sources, Related Reading, and Industry Information

It is our goal with this appendix to equip you with a beginning list of dependable, high-quality resources.

For home brewing equipment, we focus on providing hard-to-find sources and specific brand names to help you build your own affordable but high-quality brewing arsenal. The commercial section includes the brands or suppliers we recommend most highly.

We have also provided a small, selective bibliography—which, like this book, contains both basic and not-so-basic references. The coffee periodicals we list represent both industry classics, which do present information of interest to avid but non-trade coffee lovers, and a few solidly consumer-oriented newcomers.

You will no doubt notice that a detailed source list for roasted coffee itself is missing. After many months of compiling, revising, then tasting more coffees and expanding our list once again, we decided that you would best be served by an invitation to write your own. There will always be superb roasters in places we haven't had the pleasure of visiting; new ones spring up all the time. There

183

are also many, many conscientious retailers who go to considerable lengths to offer fresh, superlative coffee selections from carefully chosen roasters. We simply did not feel it was conscionable, without writing another book dedicated solely to the purpose, to pretend we could present an inclusive list.

If you have an excellent local source for coffee whose style you enjoy, by all means support them. If you lack such a resource, or seek other coffees for experimentation or as a means for evaluating local roasters, use the resources we include here to help you take the first steps—and find them.

HOME BREWING EQUIPMENT

Drip Brewers

Thermos Nissan
Route 75 East
Freeport, IL 61032
(800) 831-9242

This company produces state-of-the-art thermal servers, including the 1-quart unit with matching filter cone holder we recommend as the best manual drip brewing setup. (They also manufacture a sleek and standard-setting stainless-steel plunger pot.)

Boyd's Coffee Company
19730 N.E. Sandy Blvd.
P.O. Box 20547
Portland, OR 97220
(503) 666-4545

One of the oldest and largest roasters on the West Coast,

this company has long pursued the best in brewing technology and is valuable here as the source for the Dutch Technivorm line of home brewers.

Filters

Paper filters, of course, are ubiquitous; for the oxygen-whitened type, try a natural foods store.

Gold-washed filters can be found wherever good coffee is retailed. Any specialty coffee roaster with a well-stocked mail-order house, such as Starbucks Coffee Company (Address: P.O. Box 34067, Seattle, WA 98124-1067; Tel. (800) 782-7282), can provide you with one. Brands to look for include Gold Filter and Braun.

Coffee Presses and Vacuum Pots

Bodum
2920 Wolff St.
Racine, WI 53404
(414) 633-6450
(800) 232-6386

The world's premier manufacturer of press pots also makes an excellent vacuum pot, hand grinder, and tea pot.

Flavor-Seal Corporation
1780 Maple St.
Northfield, IL 60093
(708) 446-3550

Manufacturer of a (commercial) 1/2-gallon stainless-steel vacuum pot of very high quality.

Windward Northwest
P.O. Box 380
Clinton, WA 98236
(800) 215-3606

U.S. importer of the exquisite, expensive, and difficult-to-locate British Cona vacuum pots.

Espresso Machines

Estro, Inc.
2012 Renard Ct., Suite A
Annapolis, MD 21401
(410) 573-0562

The manufacturer of the Estro brand home espresso machines distributed through Starbucks Coffee Company, also sold under their company name, Saeco.

Milk Steamers

Milk steamers are easy to find through a knowledgeable coffee retailer or gourmet kitchen store. Good brands to look for include Pulcinella and Salton/Maxim.

Grinders

Grinders are sold virtually everywhere whole-bean coffee is retailed. Any sizeable specialty coffee mail-order supplier can also provide you with one. Brands to look for include:

Blade grinder: Krups, Bosch, private labels (including Starbucks)

Burr grinder: Bunn (electric), Zassenhaus (manual grinder)

COMMERCIAL BREWING EQUIPMENT

Drip Brewers, Vacuum Pots, and Grinders

American Metal Ware
1835 Raymond Dr.
Northbrook, IL 60062
(800) 788-1883

Now owned by the outstanding commercial grinder manufacturer, Grindmaster, American Metal Ware makes state-of-the-art drip brewing equipment.

Flavor-Seal Corporation
1780 Maple St.
Northfield, IL 60093
(708) 446-3550

Manufacturer of a (commercial) 1/2-gallon stainless-steel vacuum pot of very high quality.

Fetco, Inc.
640 Heathrow Dr.
Lincolnshire, IL 60069
(800) 338-2699

The manufacturer of superbly engineered commercial drip brewing equipment.

Espresso Machines and Espresso Grinders

Espresso Specialists, Inc.
4544 Leary Way N.W.
Seattle, WA 98107
(206) 784-9563

U.S. importer and manufacturer of the superlative La Marzocco espresso machines, and importer of Astoria and Rio commercial grinders.

Espresso Armando
26 Clinton Dr., Unit 116
Hollis, NH 03049
(603) 886-0334

The manufacturer of Armando espresso machines.

RELATED READING AND INDUSTRY INFORMATION

Selected Bibliography

Castle, Timothy James. *The Perfect Cup*. Reading, MA: Aris Books (Addison Wesley), 1991.

Davids, Kenneth. *Coffee: A Guide to Buying, Brewing & Enjoying*. Singapore: 101 Productions, 1991.

Davids, Kenneth. *Espresso: Ultimate Coffee*. Santa Rosa, CA: Cole Group, 1993

Jobin, Phillipe. *Les Cafés Produits dans le Monde*. (English translation by Natalie Wagner-Marzocca.) Le Havre: P. Jobin et Cie., 1982 (Available by mail from S.A.A.A., Boîte Postale 145, 76050 Le Havre, Cedex, France. Tel. 35-19-35-00).

Jurich, Nick. *Espresso from Bean to Cup*. Seattle: Missing Link Press, 1991.

Kummer, Corby. *The Joy of Coffee*. Shelburne, VT: Chapters Publishing, 1995.

Monaghan, Joe and Julie S. Huffaker. *Espresso! Starting and Running Your Own Specialty Coffee Business.* New York NY: John Wiley & Sons, Inc., 1996.

Sivetz, Michael. *Coffee Technology.* Reprints of this classic are available from Sivetz Coffee Enterprises, 349 SW 4th St., Corvallis, OR 97333. Tel. (503) 753-9713.

Ukers, William. *All About Coffee,* 2nd ed. Long Beach, CA: Specialty Coffee Association of America, 1993 (facsimile reprint). Tel. (800) 647-8292.

Relevant Periodicals

Many of the trade journals published within the specialty coffee world are best suited to those who wish to be exposed to the mainstream news and products of the industry. However, there are several longstanding trade publications and a few rising consumer-focused stars offering information of interest to curious coffee lovers.

Coffee Companion newsletter, a fierce and witty consumer aid published quarterly by author Kevin Sinnot. Address: P.O. Box 796, Warrenville, IL 60555. Tel. (630) 393-9010.

Coffee Journal, a lovely and eclectic magazine slated more toward coffee-loving consumers than trade insiders. Address: 212 3rd Ave. N., Suite 300, Minneapolis, MN 55401. Tel. (612) 341-2278.

Tea and Coffee Trade Journal, a long-standing trade magazine with much of interest to specialty coffee lovers. Address: 130 42nd St., New York, NY 10036.

World Coffee and Tea Magazine, also primarily a trade
magazine but, like *Tea and Coffee Trade Journal,*
containing information of interest to a wide range of
specialty coffee lovers. Address: 1801 Rockville Pike,
Suite 330, Rockville, MD 20852.

Coffee Trade Organizations

For more information about the specialty coffee industry,
pertinent events, and additional resources, contact:

Specialty Coffee Association of America
One World Trade Center
Suite 800
Long Beach, CA 90831-0800
(301) 983-8090

Coffee-Region Aid Organizations

For more information about assistance to coffee-producing
regions, or for a list of roasters, retailers, and other organizations contributing to their efforts, contact:

Coffee Kids
207 Wickenden St.
Providence, RI 02903
(401) 331-9099

INDEX